# Preface

Railways on islands always have a fascination. Due to their isolated position they develop a character of their own. The Isle of Wight is no exception. The first line opened in 1862 and by 1900 55½ miles of track had been laid by eight different companies. As the years went by the small companies joined and by 1923 the whole system was under the control of the Southern Railway.

The Isle of Wight Railway (1864-1923) managed to show a small profit but the rest struggled to survive. Two of these, The Isle of Wight Central Railway (formed in 1887 with the joining of the Cowes and Newport Railway, The Ryde and Newport Railway, The Newport Junction Railway and later the Newport, Godshill and St. Lawrence Railway) and the Freshwater Yarmouth and Newport Railway (1880-1923) feature in this book; their histories are very involved and fascinating.

Writing this book has involved the help and assistance of a number of people. First thanks must go to Peter Cooper who has been indispensible in the checking of my text. Drawings come from the pen of Colin Binnie, my brother-in-law. When he lived at Havant, some thirty years ago, many happy hours were spent with the 'Terriers' on the Hayling Island line. On the technical side guidance has come from Len Pullinger, Bob Forsythe and Jack Owen. Editors Iain Whitlam of the 'Wight Report' and Phillip Shaw of the 'Tenterden Terrier' have been of great help. Many people have contributed to the photographic illustrations, notably John L. Smith (Lens of Sutton) and John Goss.

Reference has been made to the LBSCR and IWCR records held at the Public Record Office, Kew. The main published sources have been 'Locomotives of the LBSCR, part 1' and 'A Locomotive History of the Railways of the Isle of Wight' both by the late D.L. Bradley, published by the RCTS.

Proof reading was done by Roger Macdonald of the Isle of Wight Steam Railway. Grateful thanks are due to Miss Ally Beale who typed the manuscript.

*Front cover:* The Bembridge branch was a regular 'Terrier' area of work in the early days of the Southern Railway (up to 1936). No. W13 *Carisbrooke* is coming off the branch and running into Brading station.
*Lens of Sutton*

*Back cover:* A valuable workhorse - 'Terrier' No. 8 *Freshwater* - has been prepared for a day's work on the Isle of Wight Steam Railway. The workers who have prepared the locomotive line up for a picture with the 'Terrier'.
*Roger Macdonald*

©M.J.E. Reed &
Kingfisher Railway Productions
1989
ISBN 0 946184 46 1
Typeset by
Alphaset
65a The Avenue
Southampton

Printed by
Amadeus Press
Huddersfield

# The Island Terriers

## M.J.E. Reed
### Edited by Peter Cooper

No. W8 has stopped while working one of the Shide cement quarry trains, in the mid 1930s.
*Lens of Sutton*

# Contents

Published by
## Kingfisher Railway Productions
65A The Avenue, Southampton SO1 2TA

# Introduction

The London Brighton and South Coast Railway's 'Terrier' class were designed by William Stroudley and introduced into service in 1872. They were officially the 'A' class 0-6-0 tank engines, and were later known as the 'A1' class; those rebuilt with Marsh boiler and extended smokebox, from 1911 onwards, were known as the 'A1X' class. The original batch of six 'Terriers' built in 1872 were added to during the decade, and when the class was complete in 1880 it totalled 50 locomotives, numbered 35 to 84.

The original reason for building the 'Terriers' was to work passenger trains over the lightly laid track of lines such as the South London line, from Victoria to London Bridge, a line with frequent stops and some significant gradients. They were quite small engines by the mainline standards of the 1870s, and so they look positively dimunitive to late 20th century eyes; this miniature appearance has probably contributed greatly to their celebrity over the years. They were certainly successful in their original employment on the South London line, and also on the East London line (now part of the London Transport Metropoliton line).

were sold to various new owners - railway companies, contractors, etc. This led to the acquisition of 'Terriers' by the railway companies on the Isle of Wight, and to the start of an association of the class with the Island which lasted for almost exactly 50 years, from 1899 to 1949, and which has now been re-established in preservation.

There were three main railway companies on the Isle of Wight before the 1922 Grouping of the railways. The largest was the Isle of Wight Central Railway (IWCR); this was formed in 1887 by the amalgamation of the Cowes & Newport Railway (opened in 1862, and the first railway on the Island), the Ryde & Newport Railway (opened in 1875) and the Isle of Wight (Newport Junction) Railway (opened by 1880). The IWCR thus had a system with lines from Newport to Cowes, Ryde and Sandown, with a branch from Merstone, on the Sandown line, to Ventnor Town (later renamed Ventnor West). The IWCR was operated by a remarkable variety of locomotives, but this railway later became the first, and principal, buyer of 'Terriers' on the Island, buying four of these locomotives between 1899 and 1903.

Island 'Terriers' on parade. Nos. W9, W10 and W12 lined up at Newport, in about 1930, ready for their first turns of duty.

*O.J. Morris/Lens of Sutton*

Within a few years, as the LBSCR's suburban track was relaid and enhanced, some of the suburban services the 'Terriers' had been built for had been taken over by larger locomotives, notably Stroudley's 'D' class 0-4-2 tanks. This meant that the 'Terriers' began slowly to move away from London, and to be transferred to the provincial depots of the LBSCR, such as Brighton, Eastbourne, Portsmouth and Midhurst. Eleven of the 50 'Terriers' were based in the provinces by 1884, nineteen by 1889, and twenty one by 1896. By the end of the 1890s it was becoming hard to find work for the whole 'Terrier' class, and it was officially decreed it should be reduced to a class of 15 locomotives only. Some were withdrawn and cut up, but others

The 'Terriers' were the most numerous single type owned by the IWCR, and can be regarded as the nearest thing to a standard class that the railway possessed. A part of the Ryde-Newport section of the IWCR still functions today as the Isle of Wight Steam Railway.

The second railway system on the Island was the Isle of Wight Railway (IWR), with a main line from Ryde to Ventnor, and a branch from Brading to Bembridge. The IWR opened in 1864 and was operated almost entirely by Beyer Peacock 2-4-0 tank engines. The railway never possessed 'Terriers', which had little association with its line, though they did operate the Bembridge branch in the early 1930s. The Ryde-Shanklin section of the IWR is still in operation today, as British Rail's only railway on the Island.

The smallest of the three Island railways was the Freshwater, Yarmouth & Newport Railway (FYNR), which opened in 1889 and operated a line connecting these three towns. Initially it was operated by the IWCR, but from 1913 it ran its own services, and obtained its own locomotives. It had two of these, one of which was a 'Terrier' acquired in 1913 third-hand from the LSWR, who had obtained it second-hand from the LBSCR in 1903.

This indicates the extent of the Island railways when the first 'Terrier' arrived in 1899, and all these lines were still operating when the last one left in 1949, though some closed quite soon after that. The 1922 Grouping of the railways made all these three Island railways part of the Southern Railway, which thus acquired five 'Terriers' as part of the Island railway stock. One of these five was withdrawn and cut up in the early days of the Southern, but between 1927 and 1930 the Southern sent out three more 'Terriers' to the Island. At the peak of Island 'Terrier' operations, between 1930 and 1936, seven of these locomotives were at work there, but four were sent back to the mainland in 1936, another in 1947, and the last two in 1949.

Meanwhile, on the mainland, the 'Terrier' story had continued on its intricate and fascinating way. The Southern Railway, on its formation in 1923, had inherited 16 'Terriers' from the LBSCR and seven more from other railways (including those of the Isle of Wight). Two further sales, one further acquisition, and a few withdrawals had followed in the Southern era, and British Railways had, in turn, inherited 14 'Terriers' from the Southern and three more from elsewhere. During most of the 1950s there were 13 'Terriers' in service on the Southern Region (three of them in departmental use); after this numbers reduced slightly and then this part of the story finished fairly abruptly in 1963 when their workings at Newhaven and Hayling Island ceased, and the last ones were withdrawn from service. The final withdrawals during 1963 included four 'Terriers' which had previously served on the Isle of Wight, and so feature in this book.

A few characteristics of Island 'Terriers' can be noted. All 'Terriers' had originally been named (like most of Stroudley's locomotives) but these names had been removed by the LBSCR early in the 20th century, and by the IWCR following purchase of the locomotives. In the late 1920s the Southern Railway applied names to all its Isle of Wight locomotvies, so all but one of the Island 'Terriers' had two names in the course of their working lives (a distinction they shared with all but one of the 'Terriers' sold to the Colonel Stephens railways). A feature of all Island 'Terriers' was the extended coal bunker, of much greater capacity than the Stroudley original; this modification was originally applied by the IWCR, but was later adopted by the SR as standard for Island 'Terriers'. Another Southern standard for Island locomotives in the 1930s was the LSWR Drummond pattern chimney, which was applied to all the Island 'Terriers' at that time, except the two which retained 12″ cylinders. The Drummond-chimneyed 'Terrier' was not exclusively an Isle of Wight creation, as a few mainland 'Terriers' did run with this pattern. In pregrouping days the IWCR had fitted characteristic locally manufactured chimneys to all their 'Terriers'.

The 'Terriers' were acknowledged by the Southern as one of their standard locomotive classes for Isle of Wight operations, if only for specialist lightweight duties - the ubiquitous ex-LSWR 'O2' class 0-4-4 tanks handled most of the major workings and eventually became the only locomotive class on the Island. During the Southern Railway era the principal areas of 'Terrier' operation were the Ventnor West and Bembridge branches, and the Freshwater line, plus a few local goods workings in the Newport area. The 'Terriers' were an important part of the Island railway scene, and so it is entirely fitting that two of them should be preserved on the Isle of Wight Steam Railway, where one of them has given splendidly dependable service for a number of seasons.

Eight 'Terriers' in all worked on the Isle of Wight, and each has an interesting history, so they will now be described in turn, in the order of their arrival on the Island.

Newport was the hub of much of the Island 'Terrier' activity. 'Terrier' No. W8 *Freshwater*, now preserved back on the Island, is on a typical train at Newport in the late 1930s. *Lens of Sutton*

# The First No. 9

This locomotive was the first 'Terrier' to set its wheels on Isle of Wight rails. It was also the oldest of the 'Terriers' to run on the Isle of Wight, and so is the undoubted starting point for our story. It left Brighton Works erecting shop on 25th November 1872, as the fifth 'Terrier' built, numbered 75 and named *Blackwall* (a location now famous for its road tunnel). It ran a trial journey on 1st December 1872 and entered service the next day, being shedded at New Cross, but moving to Battersea in the early 1880s. In the 1890s it left Battersea and was transferred to Brighton, from where it worked the Kemp Town Branch and also made some journeys to Hove, Lewes and Newhaven, together with some station piloting. 1897 saw the fitting of new 14″ dia cylinders and the removal of the condensing pipes, so that all the exhaust steam now went up the blast pipe to the atmosphere.

After the sale of the 'Terrier' *Fenchurch* to the Newhaven Harbour Company in June 1898, the Isle of Wight Central Railway's Board gave their approval on 14th September 1898 to Charles Conacher, their flamboyant general manager, to buy a 'Terrier' from the LBSCR, or some similar locomotive, either new or secondhand. But Conacher got a negative answer from the LBSCR. He had also written to the LSWR which offered a Manning Wardle saddle tank built in 1862, named *Lady Portsmouth* and numbered 392, at a price of £550, and an 'Ilfracombe' Goods, an 0-6-0 tender engine No. 282 built by Beyer Peacock & Co. in 1873, for an asking price of £750. If the IWCR did not require the tender then the loco would cost £685! Conacher liked the Ilfracombe Goods but to have used a long wheel base locomotive on the Island would have presented problems everywhere. The Manning Wardle of 1862 was not favoured as it was the same age as the locomotives (Nos 1 & 2, the Slaughter Grunings 2-2-2 Well Tanks) that they wished to replace. Beyer Peacock & Co. were also contacted, as the IWCR had brought a new locomotive from them earlier that year. Conacher went back to the LBSCR and on 2nd November 1898 *Blackwall* was inspected, at the IWCR's request, by J.M. Budge of the Great Northern Railway from Doncaster. He found the locomotive in good order. The price agreed was £800 (rather a high price perhaps, as *Fenchurch* was sold for £350 in June 1898 with a mileage of 599,297). The LBSCR painted *Blackwall* in IWCR red livery, with, on the side tanks, the IWCR garter with the words "Central Railway" and the number "9" in the centre. The garter measured 12¾″ wide x 14¾″ high, and its body was vermillion, the shading black and the rest gilt.

Technical details of *Blackwall* in its 1899 condition were as follows:-

| | | |
|---|---|---|
| Cylinders 14″ dia × 20″ | | |
| Heating Surface | | |
| Tubes | 118 × 1¾″ dia = | 456 sq ft |
| Firebox | | 55 sq ft |
| | Total | 511 sq ft |
| Coal bunker capacity | | 12 cwt |
| Weights in working order | | |
| Leading axle | | 7 T 15 c |
| Driving axle | | 10 T 3 c |
| Trailing axle | | 9 T 12 c |
| | Total | 27T 10 c |

and the locomotive arrived on the Island in March 1899, its LBSCR mileage being 580,982.

The newly acquired IWCR No. 9 was brought over on a lighter from Portsmouth to Medham Hard, as was usual for arriving locomotives for the IWCR. The unloading of a locomotive at Medham must have been quite a sight! The lighter with the locomotive aboard would be brought in as near to the shore as possible on the high tide, so that as the tide went out the lighter was left aground. Temporary track was then laid down and the locomotive was winched off the lighter, across the mud flats, and onto the Cowes to Newport line, which runs very close to the River Medina at this point. This landing procedure had been carried out many times since its first use in 1861. On one occasion, the unloading of 0-4-2 tank No. 3 in 1870, the locomotive fell in the mud and it took a fortnight's work to get it back onto dry land. The IWCR bought No. 9 on a hire purchase agreement with the Southern Counties Rolling Stock Finance Company, the monthly repayments being £9.8.0 over a 10 year period. The railway had clearly made a good purchase, and No. 9 was liked by the locomotive crews. Over the next four years three more 'Terriers' were bought by the IWCR; the association of 'Terriers' with the Isle of Wight was well and truly established.

The first 'Terrier' to go to the Isle of Wight began life as LBSCR No. 75 *Blackwall*. It is seen here in its pre-1897 condition, with the steam heating pipes in place.
*Lens of Sutton*

No. 75 was sent to the Island in 1899 and became Isle of Wight Central Railway (IWCR) No. 9. It ran at first in the railway's maroon 'garter' livery, as seen in this early shot.
*Lens of Sutton*

*Left:* Two IWCR liveries, and a few changes, later. No. 9 now has a Wheeler & Hurst chimney, an extended bunker, and the lined black 'IWC' livery of the railway's last years.
*Real Photographs/R.C. Riley collection*

*Below:* One of the regular 'Terrier' areas of work was the Ventnor Town branch. This line still looks quite new as No. 9 heads a train from Ventnor near St. Lawrence.
*L&GRP collection, courtesy David & Charles*

Latterly No. W9 spent some time working on the Freshwater line, and is here arriving at Freshwater station in early Southern days.

*Lens of Sutton*

On 15th June 1901 J.H. Seymour the Locomotive Superintendent (about whom we do not hear very much, although he held the post from 1895 - 1905 - but with Charles Conacher as general manager this is not so surprising!) carried out a detailed examination of all the locomotives and rolling stock of the Company. He found No. 9 in good repair except for some cracks in the back tube plate, which had had to be caulked up occasionally by the boiler maker. Another detailed examination was called for in 1904, which was not a good year for the IWCR. Locomotive shortages resulted in trains running late or being cancelled and passengers missing boats to the mainland. The Board received many complaints, and on 23rd December 1904 they instructed Charles Conacher to prepare a report on the locomotives and to have it ready for a meeting in January. But again, little was reported on No. 9 except that it had had new tyres in March 1904, and had now run a mileage of 661,322. In July 1905 J.H. Seymour obtained an appointment abroad (apparently in Southern Africa; Seymour had been in Pretoria some five years earlier), and on 28th August 1905 Robert Guest, of the LSWR was engaged as Locomotive Superintendent for four years at £4 per week, at a time when the general manager's salary was £450 per annum.

In May 1901 the IWCR brought in a livery change; the main colour remained the same (crimson) but the garter was discarded in favour of fully lettered side tanks 'ISLE OF WIGHT' in large letters with 'CENTRAL RAILWAY' in slightly smaller letters underneath, and the number moved to the coal bunker. No. 9 received this new livery later in 1901.

Early in 1908 No. 9 was called into Newport repair shop for heavy repairs. These workshops had been brought into use in March 1891, with much of the equipment bought second hand from the LSWR works at Nine Elms (London), and with a normal staff of six men and three boys. This was not a speedy workshop, and some locomotives going into it seem to have stayed there for quite a long time, a year not being uncommon.

The IWCR was a small, impecunious, independent railway, for which life was often hard; a few incidents around this time will illustrate this. On 27th April 1908 the IWCR bought a wheel press for £46 from London Bros, though the LSWR had a wheel lathe for sale for £200 - the Directors considered this too expensive; the IWCR did own a 5′0″ wheel lathe, which was installed second hand in 1891, and so was probably 40 or 50 years old. In 1908 the Board did however give Robert Guest permission to employ an apprentice for £15 to £20 per year. In 1911 the Newport, Godshill and St. Lawrence Railway (the Ventnor branch which the 'Terriers' normally worked) was in chancery, being unable to pay its interest requirements on debentures, and the shareholders were very unhappy at the continued loss on this line, which it has been said was operated in the winter months with just a conductor and a driver, without the knowledge of the Board of Trade. The winter services in 1911-1912 were reduced, particularly on the Ventnor branch which had made a loss of £6,749 between 1897 and February 1911. The IWCR was without a manager after the departure of Charles Conacher in March 1910, when he left to take up an appointment with the Cambrian Railways in Wales; George Henly, the Company's Accountant, was appointed manager and accountant on 26th April 1911 at £400 per year. At the same meeting H.F. Stephens (the famous Colonel) was appointed both Civil Engineer and Locomotive Superintendent for £100 per year, starting on 1st August 1911;

No. 9 was one of the few 'Als' ever to run in Southern green livery, as No. W9, and was the only Island 'Terrier' not to carry a name. The locomotive was still hardly changed, and is photographed during its brief SR career.                         *R.C. Riley collection*

a legendary figure of the light railway scene had walked onto the IWCR's stage, but, alas, only briefly, as he soon found that visiting the line once a week was too much for him and resigned on 30th September 1911.

On 4th April 1911 a Mr Thom from the LSWR examined all the IWCR's locomotives. He signed himself as Locomotive Superintendent though he was not, as Robert Guest remained Locomotive Superintendent until 31st July 1911. His examination of No. 9 found that the coupling rods needed rebushing, axleboxes were worn and the springs required resetting. The engine was in bad condition, requiring a thorough overhaul; the boiler had been repaired in February 1911, when it had been patched and twenty new tubes had been fitted. He recommended that the boiler should have a complete new set of tubes, and that some caulking and fullering up was needed plus an internal inspection; the estimated cost was £76.12.0. Finally, to really cheer the Directors up, No. 9 broke its crank axle in June.

Some relief was eventually found for No. 9's boiler problems. The boiler that has been taken from 'Terrier' No. 12 in March 1916, when No. 12 was converted to an 'A1X', was returned to the Brighton works of the LBSCR for rebuilding, at a cost of £184, and was then returned to the Island and fitted to No. 9 in March 1917. The boiler feed pumps were removed and injectors fitted. The chimneys on the 'Terriers' were all by now showing signs of their age and local replacements were made by Wheeler and Hurst of Newport. New 14″ cylinders, bought from the LBSCR, were fitted to No. 9 and the wooden brake blocks replaced by cast-iron.

1923 was the year of the Grouping of the railways and autumn saw the FYNR and the IWCR both under Southern Railway ownership. The FYNR's Manning Wardle tank No. 1 was transferred to work at Medina Wharf and No. 9 took over its duties on the Freshwater line. A new driving axle and wheels for No. 9 were sent over from Brighton works in February 1923, but it is believed that they were never fitted. In 1924 the

locomotive was painted in Southern Railway Maunsell green livery with the word 'SOUTHERN' high up on the side tanks, the letter 'W' in the centre and the number '9' at the bottom. Early in 1926 push-pull equipment was fitted to No. W9, but soon after this it broke a crank axle near Ningwood (on the Freshwater line), and was then damaged while awaiting repairs in Ryde Yard, on the evening of 28th March 1926.

The decision whether to repair No. W9 was delayed until April 27th, when the boiler was condemned with a faulty firebox, though the official withdrawal date on the record card shows April 1926, and the boiler was removed from the stock list in January 1927. No. W9 was moved to the Gas Works siding at St. Helens, sold for scrap and broken up. Its final mileage on the Island was 321,669, plus her LBSCR mileage of 580,982, giving a total of 902,651 miles, in just over 53 years service. This 'Terrier' had split its working life almost exactly equally between the mainland and the Island, spending just over 26 years with the LBSCR, and then about 27 years with the IWCR and SR on the Isle of Wight.

Discarded. The withdrawn No. W9 sits in the Gas Works siding at St. Helens, waiting to be broken up.

*Lens of Sutton*

# No. W10 Cowes

The Isle of Wight Central Railway's second 'Terrier' No. 10 was the eighth 'Terrier' built; originally named *Peckham* and numbered 69, it entered traffic on 9th July 1874 and was shedded at Battersea, where it remained until March 1888. In that month an accident on the Newhaven Harbour Company's railway system caused both of the company's two locomotives to be out of commission, and No. 69 was one of the two 'Terriers' sent as temporary replacements, returning to Battersea two months later.

*Peckham* was back at Newhaven again in February 1898 whilst negotiations were in progress which led to the purchase of *Fenchurch* by the Harbour Company. Agreement was reached and on 27th June 1898 *Fenchurch* began working for its new owners, so *Peckham* returned to Battersea. In April 1899 it was fitted with new 14″ dia cylinders and had its condensing pipes removed.

The IWCR was pleased with the way that No. 9 had performed and on 20th November 1899 the Board decided to buy another 'Terrier'. Early in December they asked the LBSCR if they had a 'Terrier' for sale and they were offered No. 69 *Peckham* for £700. In February 1900 Dugald Drummond, the Locomotive Superintendent of the LSWR, inspected the locomotive at Brighton and recommended that the I W C R should purchase it. The IWCR agreed to buy the locomotive on 28th February 1900, providing general repairs were carried out and that the locomotive was painted in the new IWCR livery. This having been done No. 10, as it was now numbered, crossed the Solent on 18th April 1900. It was bought on a hire purchase agreement similar to that for No. 9.

No. 69 *Peckham*, which later became IWCR No. 10.    *Lens of Sutton*

A very pleasant rural branch terminus. IWCR No. 10 runs into Ventnor Town station in the early 1900s.    *Lens of Sutton*

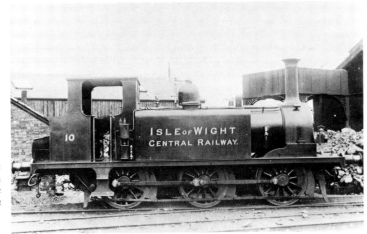

After the 'garter' livery (see No. 9) the next livery was the 'spelt out' livery of the years around 1910. No. 10, is seen at Newport in this later livery. Note the wooden brake blocks.  *Lens of Sutton*

*Left:* No. 10 took on the standard IWCR 'Terrier' appearance in the final days of independence; 'IWC' livery, locally built chimney, cast iron brake blocks and bunker extended for greater coal capacity.  *Lens of Sutton*

*Below:* A train of coal wagons proceeds towards Ryde, along the IWCR's single track near Smallbrook Junction. This is alongside the Isle of Wight Railway's single track main line, and No. 10 is in charge in the summer of 1923.
*Lens of Sutton*

A fresh livery, but the loco is little altered. No. W10 in about 1926 at Newport.
*Lens of Sutton*

J.H. Seymour the IWCR Locomotive Superintendent inspected No. 10 on 15th June 1901. He found the locomotive in good repair, and after one year on the Island it had given satisfactory service. Similarly, the December 1904 locomotive report had little to say against No. 10, except that a new crank axle had been fitted, to replace one broken in December 1902; the cost of fitting this and a new set of tyres, in April 1903, had been £120. No. W10's mileage was 647,924 at this point (71,632 on the Island). In 1909 No. 10 was in Newport shops for heavy repairs where the crank axle (fitted in 1903) was taken out and fitted into No. 12 which had broken its crank axle. No. 10 stayed in the repair shops until February 1911 - a rather lengthy duration, presumably while another new crank axle was obtained.

On 4th April 1911 when Mr. Thom carried out his inspection, the engine (that is everything except the boiler) was in good condition. But he was far from pleased with the boiler; he considered previous repairs to be most unsatisfactory and a further £32.10.0 needed to be spent. On Whit Sunday and Monday 1912 a detailed examination was made of all the IWCR locomotives by a locomotive expert and a boiler inspector, who were not named in the Company's Minutes. Rather surprisingly everything was found in a very satisfactory condition - except for minor details. About this time the IWCR Board seems to have spent a great deal of time discussing locomotive coal and its cost; they found that a typical coal and price was Mansfield coal bought at 19 shillings (95p) per ton in December 1913.

The western extremity of the Island railway system. No. W10 running round a train at Freshwater in June 1928.
*H.F. Wheeller*

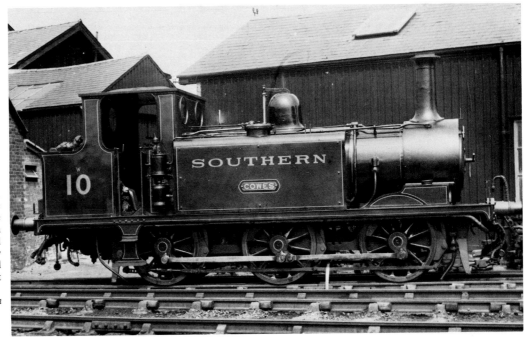

No. W10 was rebuilt to 'AIX' in 1930, and received a Marsh chimney. The name *Cowes* was applied about the same time. Fitted for steam heating and push-and-pull operation, and looking very smart in Southern lined green, at Newport in about 1930.
*O.J. Morris/Lens of Sutton*

Some modifications were made to the locomotive about this time. In common with other 'Terriers' on the IWCR, No. 10 had its coal bunker enlarged to hold 1½ tons, the wooden brake blocks were replaced by cast iron, and it received one of Wheeler and Hurst's new tapered chimneys. New 14″ diameter cylinders were fitted in June 1915, and injectors replaced her ageing boiler feed pumps. Following the formation of the Southern Railway in 1923, No. 10 was painted Maunsell green livery in 1925 and became W10. February 1926 saw the fitting of push-pull gear, of the pattern used on the Ventnor West line after 1925; No. 10 had spent most of its time on that branch until 1924, when it took turns on the Freshwater line. Steam heating gear was fitted to No. W10 in October 1927.

A.B. MacLeod (the new Assistant for the Isle of Wight) decided that engines ought to have names (the author agrees), and allocated No. W10 the name *Cowes* in October 1928, although its bronze nameplates were not fitted until April 1930. Its original 1874 'A1' boiler was condemned in February 1930, and it was rebuilt into an 'A1X' at Ryde Works with a boiler taken from No. W12 (boiler No. 1094, new in July 1916) and was fitted with a Marsh Chimney. The gravity fed sandbox splashers were retained (as on Nos. W11 and W12). No. W10 then continued to work on the Ventnor West line, but in May 1936 it left the Island for Eastleigh Works and was stored in the paint shop until 8th April 1940. It was moved to the works dump, robbed of many parts to keep the other 'Terriers' running and finally broken up at the end of March 1949.

The scrap road. No. W10 many years later, in final condition at Eastleigh, but with some vital parts removed. 10th April 1948.
*J.H. Aston*

# No. W11 Newport

After describing two relatively little known, and long departed, 'Terriers', we now come to a very celebrated 'Terrier', and one which happily is still with us. This 'Terrier's' fame began early in its life, but it has a special place in the Island 'Terrier' story, as it worked on the Island for longer than any other 'Terrier'. This means it is particularly good to be able to record that the locomotive is now back on the Island, and is being returned to running order.

This famous 'Terrier' was completed on 10th March 1878, the 37th of the class to leave the erecting shops, but it was not destined to enter service straight away. Named *Brighton* and numbered 40, it was elaborately painted and sent to the Paris Exhibition of 1878, the ''Exposition Universelle''. The choice of the 'Terrier' rather than any other locomotive was governed by the lifting ability of the largest available crane, which was the 25 ton crane at Portsmouth.

*Brighton's* first trail run was on 27th March 1878; the driver was George Aylwin, the man chosen to drive the engine in France. All must have gone well, as the next day the locomotive ran to Portsmouth, and on arrival was loaded onto the LBSCR's own vessel *Honfleur*, a 269 ton, single screw, three masted cargo vessel built in 1877 by Gourlay Brothers of Dundee. Owing to bad weather the departure was delayed until 30th March, when the ship set sail for Newhaven to take on more cargo. William Stroudley also joined the ship, together with John Jeffery, the manager of the Brighton Locomotive Works and Evan Cameron, the head of the Carriage Department. The ship crossed the Channel during the night, arriving at Dieppe in the morning of Sunday 31st March. *Brighton* was unloaded, steamed and ran light to Paris with the assistance of a French pilotman and fireman. There the 'Terrier' was shedded at St. Lazare, near the terminus of the Chemin de Fer de l'Ouest, (the Western Railway of France).

The exhibition was not due to open until 1st May and the British stand in the motion section of the machinery hall was far from ready. Other companies' plans for the exhibition were not running smoothly, either. The Westinghouse Brake Company of America, exhibiting their continuous brake system for the first

*Above:* The great man himself. William Stroudley stands beside No. 40 *Brighton* in 1878 shortly after the locomotive's return from its triumphant visit to Paris.          *Lens of Sutton*

*Left:* The prizewinning 'Terrier'. *Brighton* with the Paris gold medal award recorded on the tank sides for all to see. This is another of the celebratory photos taken after its return from Paris.
                *Lens of Sutton*

The platform end at Newport, with distinctive footbridge, was a favourite point for photographing locomotives for many years. *Brighton* has become IWCR No. 11, and has the final, lined black, livery, but retains a form of the original copper capped chimney. So this is probably about 1915.

*Lens of Sutton*

time in Europe, had problems. Although the LBSCR had adopted this system, Westinghouse wanted to demonstrate it, and Driver Aylwin was approached with a request to borrow *Brighton*; Aylwin consulted Stroudley who agreed. The 'Terrier' made many runs in and around Paris, Westinghouse were very pleased with the results, and the French engineers were very impressed with the way the locomotive handled the train. The locomotive was then displayed in the exhibition together with a piston, piston rod, connecting rod and other items which had completed 185,446 miles running. In October 1878 the judging of the exhibits took place. Prize day was on Monday 21st October and the British received a total of 270 gold medals which were distributed in the middle of 1879; one was awarded to *Brighton* for its design, workmanship and finish.

The prize winning 'Terrier' then went back to Dieppe for shipment to England, and on her return Stroudley arranged for a series of photographs to be taken by Mr. E.J. Bedford, the assistant art master at the Brighton School of Art. At a directors' meeting on 18th June the medal was put on display; the directors agreed that it should be presented to Stroudley, and this presentation took place on 2nd July 1879. For a while Stroudley used this engine for experimental work. His patent speed indicator was fitted, a version of which may be seen in the Science Museum in London; March 1887 saw steam sanding gear fitted, and in October 1887 patent iron boiler tubes were fitted, and later a variable blast pipe. During this period No. 40 carried out normal duties, being shedded at Battersea. New 14″ cylinders were fitted in January 1894, and the condensing pipes were removed, but in 1901 the locomotive left for Newhaven to help with sea defence work, and when this work was finished *Brighton* was found surplus to requirements.

At this time the IWCR was looking for a third 'Terrier' and on 20th November 1901 the sale was agreed at £600 with 522,583 miles run. As a condition of sale the LBSCR agreed to fit

No. 11 was rebuilt to 'AIX' in 1918, the third of the three non-LBSCR 'Terriers' so rebuilt. The locomotive has also acquired familiar features - the extended bunker and Wheeler & Hurst chimney. Newport, about 1920.

*Lens of Sutton*

Island 'Terrier' at work; No. 11 arrives at Alverstone. The date is allegedly June 1919, though some of the intending passengers seem a bit overdressed for 'flaming' June.

*Lens of Sutton*

a reconditioned set of 13″ cylinders and to paint the locomotive in the metallic crimson lake livery of the IWCR for another £35.16.0. LBSCR No. 40 now became IWCR No. 11, which was bought under a hire purchase agreement with the Southern Counties Rolling Stock Finance Company as with the two previous IWCR 'Terriers'; No. 11 arrived on the Isle of Wight on 8th January 1902. Coal bunker rails were added in October 1904 and by then it had run 78,421 miles in 2 years 9 months on the Island. The coal rails were not popular although they gave greater coal capacity, which reduced the number of times a locomotive required to leave its train to visit the coaling stage for more coal. Visability running bunker first was greatly reduced. It was decided to move the tool box and extend the bunker to the buffer beam; this gave a coal capacity of 1½ tons, although it was not done until 1918 on this locomotive. The engine was also in shops undergoing repairs from January 1909 to December 1909.

On 4th April 1911 Mr. Thom from the LSWR inspected No. 11, and mechanically the engine was found to be sound, except for badly worn axle boxes. The boiler was showing signs of wear; the lower parts of the firebox were only 1/16″ thick in places ('A1' boilers were built of 7/16″ thick boiler plate) and a patch that had been put on the back plate of the firebox did not meet with Mr. Thom's approval. In his opinion the firebox was in a dangerous condition. He suggested that:- "The tubes should be taken out. The boiler barrel thoroughly cleaned and examined internally. Provided it is found good, two ½″ thick copper side plates should be fitted to the firebox and a ¾″ thick copper back plate. The firebox restayed and the engine thoroughly overhauled and boiler tested by hydraulic pressure to 180lbs P.S.I. and by steam to 145lbs P.S.I. Provided new tubes are fitted to

the boiler I estimate the cost of repairs will be about £130''. This sounded a lot of money to the IWCR, but on 28th June 1911 the engine went into the works and stayed there for four weeks, afterwards returning to service mainly on the Ventnor West line.

The next big milestone in this 'Terrier's' long life was in July 1918. A new boiler, No. 1111, built by the LBSCR at a cost of £1,195, was fitted at Newport, making No. 11 into an 'A1X'. The Isle of Wight rebuilds differ from the mainland rebuilds, as they retain the sandbox front splashers, whereas the mainland rebuilds had a new cast splasher with larger sandboxes fitted under the footplate. New 13″ cylinders were also purchased from the LBSCR at a cost of £50. These were fitted, together with injectors replacing the worn out feed pumps, and also a locally cast chimney from Wheeler and Hurst's of Newport. No. 11 was painted in the new IWCR livery, deep glossy back with vermillion panelling and white lining, with the side tanks lettered 'I.W.C.' in gilt with brown shading. On Saturday 3rd July 1920 No. 11 was hauling the 1.24 pm. Saturdays only passenger train from Ryde Pier Head, when the trailing axle broke whilst approaching Ryde St. Johns, damaging the permanent way for about 45 yards. An examination disclosed a flaw in the axle which had not been noticed when the engine was overhauled during the winter, so a new axle was ordered from the LBSCR and fitted at Newport.

In 1924 No. 11 had another livery change as its new owners, the Southern Railway, painted it Maunsell green and numbered it W11. Like the other ex-IWCR 'Terriers', it was fitted with push-pull train control equipment in early 1926 and October 1927 saw the fitting of steam heating equipment. A boiler change took place in December 1927; the boiler that had been fitted new to No.

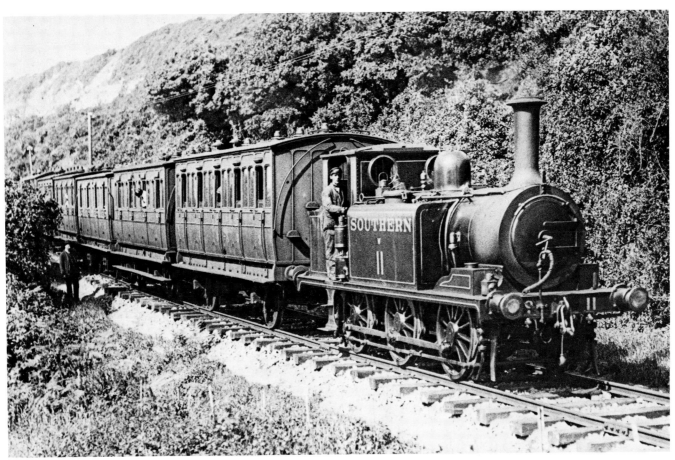

Now SR No. W11, the locomotive is at work on the Ventnor West line, on the Undercliff section, about 1925. *Lens of Sutton*

Now named *Newport*, but still retaining the Wheeler & Hurst chimney, No. W11 is ready to depart from Newport for Freshwater on 11th November 1930, with ex-LBSCR Stroudley set No. 496. *Lens of Sutton*

663 in May 1913, boiler No. BE1014 (now on *Fenchurch* on the Bluebell Railway), was tested, sent over to the Island, and fitted to No. W11, whose old boiler went to No. W12 in December 1929. In October 1928 No. W11 was allocated the name *Newport* and in June 1930, whilst undergoing repairs at Ryde Works, bronze nameplates were fixed on the side tanks. *Newport* remained working the Bembrige branch and the Ventnor West line, and in common with most Island 'Terriers' had a Drummond chimney fitted in 1932. Another boiler change took place in July 1933; boiler No. 186 (formerly numbered 934) built in 1911, came from No. W13 from which it had been removed in May 1932. In 1936 *Newport* was again in shops for repairs, and about this time front footsteps and handrails at the leading end of the side tanks were fitted. June 1939 saw *Newport* in Ryde Works again for a general overhaul and yet another boiler change. It was fitted with boiler No. 1226, built in March 1932 and previously used to convert No. W8 to an 'A1X'. No. W11 was stored at Ventnor in September 1939 for the winter, and during the war it worked the Ventnor West line, remaining in Maunsell green livery throughout the war. On 22nd April 1946 it was taken out of service in poor condition and stored at Newport. After delivering the LBSCR 0-6-2 tank No. 2510 to Medina Wharf on 22nd February 1947, the floating crane returned to Southampton with W11 and W29 *Alverstone* (an LSWR 'O2' Class for repair at Eastleigh).

At Eastleigh No. W11 was overhauled and painted in unlined black. It was stripped of the name and Island number, and given the number 2640, the number it would have carried by this time if it had remained on the mainland. In July 1947 it was returned to traffic, and after shunting at Winchester for a week was transferred to Fratton shed for Hayling Island branch duties. This 'Terrier' moved about more than most in the next few years, being transferred to Rolvenden, on the Kent & East Sussex Railway in 1948, then to Newhaven in 1951 and back to Fratton in 1954. In March 1951 it was repainted at Eastleigh and renumbered 32640 in British Railway lined black livery. In November 1958 it received its final general overhaul with British Railways, and received the final pattern BR Crest. The boiler which was fitted at this overhaul is the one that is still on the engine, No. BE 967, built at Brighton in 1912 for the first batch of 'A1Xs' and fitted new to No. 653 in May 1912. When Fratton shed closed on 2nd November 1959, No. 32640 was transferred to Eastleigh and remained working the Hayling Line until May 1963. It was then transferred home to Brighton to work as a coal stage pilot, but on 28th September 1963 it was withdrawn and was to be broken up at Eastleigh in February 1964.

This was postponed and in May 1964, Sir Billy Butlin bought three 'Terriers' including No. 32640, which was repainted yellow and went to Butlins Camp at Pwllheli, North Wales, in July 1964, where it sat as a static exhibit. In 1971 Sir Peter Allen, president of the Wight Locomotive Society, persuaded Sir Billy Butlin to agree to have No. 32640 exhibited on loan on the Isle of Wight Steam Railway for ten years. The move by road was completed on 27th January 1973 and thus the engine crossed the Solent for the third time. With modern technology it was a simple matter of driving the low loader with the locomotive aboard straight onto the vehicle ferry. The 'Terrier' was delivered to the Ryde Works of British Rail, where the idea was to restore it to working order; this had to be abandoned on account of labour and other difficulties, and the locomotive was finally conveyed to the Haven Street base of the Isle of Wight Steam Railway on 17th January 1975.

A Drummond chimney was fitted to No. W11 in about 1932, and so this picture at Newport must be in the mid 1930s, before the front steps were fitted but after the 'W' prefix was painted out.

*Lens of Sutton*

Back on the mainland, No. W11 was renumbered 2640, and worked at first on the Hayling Island branch. No. 2640 is seen waiting to leave Hayling Island terminus on a basic train.

*P. Cooper collection*

Renumbered 32640 by British Railways, and back on the Hayling Island branch again, the locomotive is at Havant on 10th April 1951; it had recently received BR lined black, with the earlier BR crest.

*A.G. Ellis*

Final BR days, and now carrying the second pattern of crest. No. 32640 returned to Brighton for its last few working months, and is seen there on 22nd April 1963.

*P.H. Groom*

Back on the Island again! The first 'Terrier' on the Isle of Wight for over 20 years arrives at Fishbourne on 27th January 1973.     *John Goss*

No. 32640 was soon repainted as IWCR No. 11, and here the externally restored locomotive has just been unveiled by Sir Peter Allen, one of the vice-Presidents of the Wight Locomotive Society, on 24th August 1975.     *John Goss*

The first locomotive into the new workshop building at Haven Street. The frames of 'Terrier' No. 11 being ceremonially pushed in on 3rd January 1981.
*Iain Whitlam*

The 'Terrier' was restored externally to its 1920 condition, with a fibreglass IWC chimney taking the place of the Drummond chimney which had been carried for the past 43 years. The unauthentic frontsteps and handrails were also removed. It was painted in IWCR lined black, numbered 11 and was unveiled by Sir Peter Allen on 24th August 1975 as part of the Ryde and Newport Railway Centenary celebrations. Also present were Mr. A.B. MacLeod and a large group of members of the Steam Railway. During 1976 the Wight Locomotive Society purchased No. 11 from Sir Billy for £3,500, and No. 11 is now the only IWCR locomotive in existence.

In 1978 a start was made to return No. 11 to a fully operational locomotive; it was obvious that this would take a lot of effort and a great deal of money. Great difficulty was experienced in dismantling this locomotive due to the time it had spent in the salty air at North Wales. For instance, a single nut could sometimes take a day to remove. Twenty one weeks were spent removing the eight bolts and splitting the two flanges of the main steam pipe. With the two air reservoirs removed, the main one passed the hydraulic test but the auxiliary failed due to corrosion. Stripping down old locomotives is rewarding if one likes looking for numbers. Generally most parts of a locomotive are numbered and if there is more than one item per locomotive its position is usually indicated. The four eccentric straps on No. 11 are numbered 40,55,78 and 80 presumably indicating the 'Terriers' they were first used on. Unfortunately quite a few parts were found to be missing. A search was started to locate and acquire an air brake duplex gauge of the LBSCR butterfly pattern, and at the time of writing the search is still going on.

Removing the cylinders proved to be a herculean task which took a year to complete, and the left hand cylinder and piston were found to be broken. In October 1979 the cylinder block was welded and machined by Messrs. Barrimar at a cost of £2,720 plus VAT. A wooden pattern was made so that a new piston could be cast. The piston has now been cast and machined and is ready for fitting. The tubes were also reluctant to leave the boiler, some taking as long as three hours instead of the usual three minutes. It must be realised that a preserved railway must give preference to its running locomotives and stock and projects like the overhauling of No. 11 must take second place. The summer of 1979 Ray Maxfield (who was then in charge of motive power), thought that No. 11 could be running within two years if the necessary finance was available and the missing parts could be obtained. But when 'Terrier' No. W8 was acquired (see later) all the available effort was switched to it, so a 'Terrier' was indeed running within two years but it was not No. 11. Up until this point all work at Haven Street had been done in the open, but it was decided that no more work would be done until the workshop was finished.

On 3rd January 1981 No. 11 was pushed into the new workshop, and work could now start again in earnest. An early task was refacing the valve port seats of the cylinder blocks. A chimney of the Wheeler and Hurst design was ordered from a foundry at Barking. The frames were cleaned by pneumatic needle guns right back to bare metal (revealing some useful datum marks) and were then painted. By the summer of 1983 it was estimated that a further £7000 would be needed to get No. 11 back into running order.

The 1912 boiler was in surprisingly good condition. The boiler inspector did however find one rivet that he did not like and the author helped to get the offending rivet out. The boiler was completely cleaned with pneumatic needle guns right back to bare metal and then painted. This job, like many other jobs, was done by the ladies of the Society.

By the Spring of 1984 the engine frames had been lowered onto the driving and trailing axles, complete with newly overhauled axleboxes and springs. The leading axle was left out to make it easier to refit the cylinder blocks. There are seven fitted bolts along the top of each cylinder and seven along the bottom, each side had a total of 28 bolts. The smoke box has to be rivetted on, with seven rivets each side, eight front and back, thirty in total, although some of these rivets might be replaced by nuts and bolts. Another job is the renewal of the 22 ¾″ B.S.W. studs holding the dome on. The ¾″ B.S.W. threads in the boiler have to be drilled out and tapped 1″ B.S.W. Also, 22 new studs 1″ B.S.W. at one end and ¾″ B.S.W. at the other have to be made and fitted.

Although work was progressing well, under the direct supervision of Len Pullinger, a great deal had still to be done. With the completion of the machine shop facilities which comprise - a 6″ screw cutting lathe, vertical mill, power saw, drills, forge and cutting and welding equipment - most jobs could now be done at Haven Street. Three-phase power was not available due to the railway's isolated position, so a diesel generator has been installed to supply electricity to drive the machine tools. The Isle of Wight Steam Railway also owns a large lathe (donated by British Gas) which is to be installed when time and money allows. Most of the time the Isle of Wight Steam Railway's locomotives *Calbourne* and *Invincible* require very little attention so that time can be devoted to the two 'Terriers', although No. W8, being an operational loco, must come first.

In October 1985 the cylinders were fitted back into the frames. In Spring 1986 the wheels were refitted, new bunker side sheets were made and fitted, the cab roof was repaired and feedwater heating connections on the cylinders were blanked off. During the summer the tanks were patched and painted inside and out, and in November 1986 the boiler was hydraulically tested. Unfortunately the test failed owing to water seepage from the dome saddle plate.

In Spring 1987 metallurgical investigation of the dome saddle plate revealed it is of wrought iron and a decision was made, in conjunction with the insurance inspector, to proceed with a welded repair. During 1987 and 1988 various works on No. 11 continued, and providing the welding of the boiler is successfully completed it is hoped that the locomotive will return to service in 1989.

Mileages run by No. 11:-

| | | |
|---|---:|---:|
| LB & SCR | 522 | 583 |
| I.W.C.R. | 198 | 746 |
| S.R. (I.O.W.) | 294 | 601 |
| 1947-63 Mainland | 148 | 794 |
| Total | 1,164 | 724 |

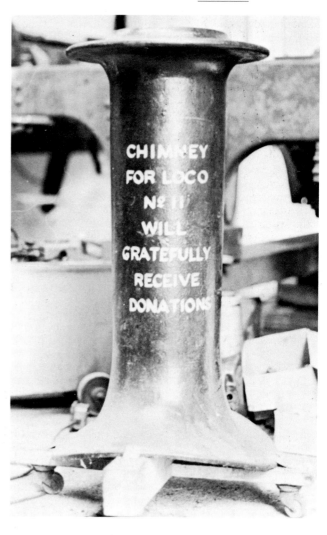

*Above:* No. 11's new chimney, making itself useful. *Author*

*Left:* The lady boilersmiths. Ally Beale and Barbara Pullinger clean the outside of No. 11's boiler with needle guns; 3rd September 1983.

*Roger Macdonald*

20

# No. W12 Ventnor

This is another of the lesser known 'Terriers'; it was the last of the class to be completed and was originally named *Crowborough* and numbered 84; it entered traffic on 8th September 1880 and was shedded at New Cross. In the mid 1880's it was transferred to Newhaven, and from there it worked the Seaford line, with some journeys to Brighton.

On 22nd June 1903 the IWCR decided that it would require a fourth Terrier, and on 22nd July 1903 the LBSCR offered them No. 671 *Wapping*, for £700. This was rejected by the IWCR because of the poor condition of the cylinders and firebox, but it was however sold to the Kent and East Sussex Railway in June 1905. Further enquiries in August 1903 resulted in the LBSCR offering No. 84 *Crowborough* for £725. The IWCR liked this engine but thought the price was too high, and during September and October attempts were made to have it reduced by £100, without success. £700 was then offered by the IWCR; the LBSCR pointed out that the engine had just been overhauled and fitted with new tyres. In the end the full £725 was paid, on 7th November 1903, and the engine left the Brighton works on the 20th November 1903, with a new blast pipe fitted and the engine painted in the red livery of the IWCR. The financial arrangements for buying No. 12 were also a little involved. The IWCR had sold all its locomotives to the Southern Counties Rolling Stock Finance Company and then hired them back. The IWCR Board had given the engineer permission to break up for scrap Nos. 1 and 2, the 1861 single wheelers, but the Company did not own the locomotives and so they could not be broken up. To overcome this problem, No. 12 was bought by the IWCR and then sold to the Finance Company, while locomotives Nos. 1 and 2 were bought by the IWCR from the Finance Company and then scrapped.

In the December 1904 report on the condition of the locomotives, No. 12 was found in good condition with a total mileage of 633,197; it had thus covered nearly 20,000 miles in its first year on the Island. In 1909 No. 12 suffered a broken crank axle, and as No. 10 was in shops undergoing repairs, No. 10's

crank axle, which was new in April 1903, was transferred to No. 12. In the same year the LBSCR contacted the IWCR with the offer of an 'E1' 0-6-0 tank locomotive No. 148 for £1000 and also two more 'Terriers' No. 80 and No. 83 for £650 each, plus delivery and any repairs that would be necessary. Instead the IWCR bought a totally unsuitable 0-4-4 tank locomotive from the North Eastern Railway, although when they sold it some 8 years later a profit of £350 was realised.

On 4th April 1911 when Mr. Thom from the LSWR inspected No. 12 he found the locomotive in a very poor state, as apparently very little work had been done on it since it had come to the Island some 7½ years earlier. The boiler was the original one, now 31 years old, and would require £96 to make it serviceable. The cylinders were coming to the end of their life and the engine was in a very bad state of repair. A major overhaul was recommended. At this time the engine was employed solely on shunting duties between Newport and Medina Wharf, except on Saturdays when it assisted with the evening market traffic. On 8th May 1911 Mr. Thom wrote the Chairman of the IWCR Board (Harry Willmott) the following memo:-

"In view of the four boilers of No. 9, 10, 11 and 12 supplied by the LBSCR being over 30 years old, I requested Mr. Henley to write to the LBSCR asking whether they could supply a second hand boiler suitable for these engines and what would be the cost. In the event of their being able to supply a new or second hand boiler perhaps you will forward the print to me, when I will get out the quantities and let you have an estimate of what it would cost to obtain a new boiler from a locomotive builder."

The letter was sent on 11th May 1911; the IWCR was a poor railway and the idea of buying spare boilers must have given the new Chairman sleepless nights.

In July 1916 (Mileage 897,589) No. 12 had a brand new 'A1X' boiler fitted (No. BE 1094) at a cost of £1195. The work of installing this boiler was carried out at Newport. As on No. 11, the rebuild was not exactly the same as the Brighton ones; the leading splashers and sandboxes were retained whereas the

The future No. W12 in its original form as LBSCR No. 84 *Crowborough* in the mid 1890s.
*Lens of Sutton*

Double heading at Newport. This must be after the 1923 Grouping as the train engine, No. W8 (not the 'Terrier' W8, of course), is in the Southern livery. No. 12, now an 'AIX', is in the standard latter condition for an IWCR 'Terrier' - locally manufactured chimney, extended bunker and lined black livery.

*Courtesy NRM, York*

The definitive photograph of No. W12 *Ventnor*. At Newport, probably in 1930, the locomotive is now in Southern livery and is named, but otherwise still looks much the same.

*O.J. Morris/Lens of Sutton*

In about 1932 No. W12 received a Drummond chimney and this took on its final appearance. As a minor detail, the 'W' prefix is no longer carried, the locomotive is seen at Newport in the mid 1930s.

*Lens of Sutton*

Brighton rebuilds had new sandboxes fitted below the running plate and new cast iron splashers. The wooden brake blocks were replaced by cast iron. A new chimney of cast iron made lo-ly at the foundry of Wheeler and Hurst was also fitted. The tool box behind the coal bunker was extended to take 1½ tons of coal. Injectors replaced the feed pumps and new 14″ diameter cylinders bought from the LB&SCR were also fitted. The locomotive was painted in the new livery of deep glossy black with vermillion panelling and fine white lining, 'I.W.C.' on the side tanks in gilt and '12' on the bunker. It is difficult to imagine that most of Europe was at war at this time. The old boiler, built in 1880, was returned to Brighton for rebuilding, and on its return it was fitted to No. 9 (see earlier).

The Southern Railway took over the IWCR officially on 1st February 1923. In May 1925 the Newport works closed and all locomotive repairs were then done at Ryde, No. 12 being the last engine to receive heavy repairs and a repaint (in Maunsell green) at Newport. The number was changed to W12, train control equipment was fitted in February 1926 enabling it to work push-pull services on the Ventnor West line, and carriage steam heating equipment was added in October 1927. In 1927 No. W12 was borrowed by Ryde shed for temporary use on the Bembridge branch, due to the scrapping of No. 5, the 2-4-0 Beyer Peacock tank. The name *Ventnor* was allocated in October 1928 and in May 1929 bronze nameplates were fitted. December 1929 saw the boiler changed; the boiler that had been fitted to No. W11 in July 1918 had been removed in December 1927 and was now reconditioned and fitted to No. W12. On returning to service No. W12 went back to work the Bembridge branch along with No. W11. 1932 saw the fitting of a Drummond chimney (of LSWR 'B4' class pattern), but with the upgrading of the Freshwater line and the Bembridge branch, together with the transfer of more LSWR 'O2' class locomotives to the Island, No. W12 was laid aside in October 1935.

The locomotive left the Island in May 1936 for Eastleigh, where it stood in the paintshop until October 1940, when it was transferred to the works dump. There it was cannibalised, and the remains were cut up during the week ending 2nd April 1949.

'Terrier' and wheels. The *Ventnor* nameplates have been removed, and No. W12 sits at Newport on 14th April 1936, waiting to be sent back to the mainland.

*S.W. Baker*

# No. W8 Freshwater

To the younger generation this is probably the best known of all the Island 'Terriers', due mainly to the work that it has done on the Isle of Wight Steam Railway since 1981. It also has the distinction of having had more owners than any other Island 'Terrier' - eight, from the LBSCR to the Wight Locomotive Society.

It was the 30th 'Terrier' to be built, named *Newington* and numbered 46. On 10th January 1877 it entered traffic, being shedded at Battersea (a shed which once boasted 21 'Terriers'), and it would appear that it stayed there until March 1903. Its usual duties included working the West London Extension Railway from Clapham Junction to Kensington (Olympia). In the 26 years and 2 months it was shedded at Battersea its average yearly mileage was 22,000 which would indicate that it was a reliable engine. New 14″ cylinders were fitted in 1896, and the feedwater heating pipes were removed.

*Newington* was renumbered 646 on 12th April 1902. In December 1902 the LSWR asked if they could buy a 'Terrier'. Their Locomotive Superintendent, Dugald Drummond, who had inspected No. 69 *Peckham* for the IWCR at Brighton in 1900, knew 'Terriers' well, being a pupil of Stroudley's. On 21st January 1903 Drummond received permission to inspect 'Terriers' working, and a few days later two of his inspectors were seen on the 7.10 am Victoria to Stoats Nest (renamed Coulsdon North in 1911) with seven bogie coaches pulled by No. 668 *Clapham*; they were very impressed. On 4th March 1903 Drummond recommended

the purchase of No. 668 *Clapham* and No. 646 *Newington* at a cost of £500 each and so on 12th March 1903 the LBSCR delivered the two Battersea locos with their names on the side tanks. Their LBSCR mileages were: 646 - 574,266 and 668 - 611,070.

At Nine Elms the Westinghouse brake, together with the Brighton works plates were removed and vacuum injectors were fitted. The locomotives were painted in Drummond livery and fully lined out; No. 646 became LSWR No. 734, and No. 668 became LSWR No. 735. No. 734 had 14″ diameter cylinders and no feedwater heating pipes, whilst No. 735 had 13″ diameter cylinders and feedwater heating pipes. The work plates removed from the front splashers were said to have been used by Drummond as paper weights in the inspection locomotive *The Bug*. On 2nd May 1903 the two 'Terriers' were sent to Guildford for local piloting duties.

The reason for buying the 'Terriers' was to provide motive power for the Lyme Regis Branch, completed in July 1903 between Axminster and Lyme Regis. It took three years to build, for a total cost of £67,000, which was remarkably cheap. Needless to say the line abounded with steep gradients of up to 1 in 40, and sharp curves down to 10 chains radius. Up to 31st December 1906 the line was owned by the Axminster and Lyme Regis Light Railway Company but operated by the LSWR who took over the line in 1907. Finding suitable engines to work the line caused some problems; the engines would have to be light on their feet

LBSCR 'Terrier' No. 646 *Newington* as delivered to the LSWR. The locomotive had just been bought for use on the Lyme Regis branch, and is seen as delivered to Nine Elms on 12th March 1903.
*Collection of the late George Kerley*

because of axle load limit of 12 tons maximum, pull well (high tractive effort) and maintain it (steam well) for up to 20 minutes at a time, covering some 4½ miles uphill. Finally the engines should be flexible enough to work round ten chain curves. In the author's view the 'Terrier', with its 12′ 0″ rigid wheelbase, is totally unsuitable for lines having curves of 10 chains or less. This is borne out on the Bembridge Branch, an almost level line of 2 miles and 65 chains which had many curves including six of 10 chains and two of 9 chains. According to Sid Newberry (The Isle of Wight Steam Railway Permanent Way Consultant) 'Terriers' used to knock the curves out badly on this branch.

Jim Wheeler, who used to be the Ganger on the Bembridge branch when the 'Terriers' worked the line, used to wag his finger at 'Mad' Jack Sturgess for high speed running, although most drivers were guilty on their duty finishing trips. Beseley curve required constant attention, and the Permanent Way Department was very pleased when the LSWR 'O2' Class locomotives took over the working of the line in May 1936. Although in Newhaven Docks (in Sussex) 'Terriers' worked round 10 chain curves, on the I.O.W. 'Terriers' had their leading and trailing wheels turned to a standard 'A' profile (now known as P1), whilst the centre wheels were turned to a standard 'G' profile. The centre wheels at Newhaven were probably standard 'E' (Now P9).

The LSWR decided that the two 'Terriers' would be ideal and the third engine would be the old LSWR '330' Class locomotive No. 131 which was used to build the line. This engine would be used as the spare engine. After six weeks at Guildford the two 'Terriers' went to Bournemouth via the Alton line. They were used for about a month on the tramway at Poole, and then went to Exmouth Junction shed, the major depot in the Lyme Regis area. Trial runs were made over the Lyme Regis branch in early August 1903, and a special train was run to inspect the line, hauled by Nos. 734 and 735, on 24th August 1903. The service commenced on 24th August 1903, with a journey time of 25 minutes at an average speed of 16½ mph. During the winter months one engine could handle the traffic, being stabled overnight at Lyme Regis in a small shed. But by August 1905 the holiday services were getting beyond the 'Terrier's' capabilities, and an 'O2' class tank was called in to give assistance. After September 1905 the 'Terriers' monopolised the line once again, but in 1906 'O2' No. 228 arrived at Lyme Regis for trials. It proved better than the 'Terriers', and so when the holiday season arrived 'O2s' were in charge, assisted by No. 735. In July 1906 No. 734 had left the area and was working the Yeovil Junction to Yeovil Town trains, while in August 1906 it was on station pilot

duties at Bournemmouth. In May 1907 'O2s' Nos. 177, 202 (later W29 *Alverstone* and 228 were working the Lyme Regis Branch, and the 'Terriers' had left completely.

The 'Terriers' were displaced and other work had to be found for them. No. 735 was soon back in steam, but No. 734 was out of service until September 1907, when it went to Eastleigh to work the Botley to Bishops Waltham branch. Early 1908 saw No. 735 at Exmouth for shunting and goods traffic to and from the Harbour, and in October it went to Bournemouth for light duties. It was then laid aside until December 1911 when it went to Eastleigh for reboilering, followed by No. 734.

Two new boilers were ordered, and in February 1912 the LSWR decided to make the boilers themselves rather than buy them from the LBSCR. They were Drummond pattern boilers having directly loaded safety valves in the dome top. The boiler dimensions were:-

| | |
|---|---|
| Boiler diameter | 3′ 4½″ |
| Boiler length | 7′ 9½″ |
| Firebox length | 4′ 0½″ |
| Grate area | 11¼ sq ft |
| Working pressure | 150lb per sq in |
| Heating surfaces | |
| Tubes | 424 sq ft |
| Firebox | 53 sq ft |
| Total | 477 sq ft |

(The author believes that these boilers had 121 × 1¾″ diameter tubes.)

| Weights in working order: | |
|---|---|
| Leading wheels | 7 T 6 c |
| Centre wheels | 9 T 17 c |
| Trailing wheels | 9 T 0 c |
| | 26 T 3 c |

The boiler for No. 734 was later numbered 184 (by the Southern Railway) and December 1912 was given as date built; it was fitted in September 1912, together with train steam heating equipment. These boilers were poor steamers and primed badly (water coming out with steam). Reconditioned crank axles were purchased from the LBSCR, one of them coming from No. 76 *Hailsham*. Both engines received new 13″ diameter cylinders cast and machined at Eastleigh, and new blast pipes were fitted. The LBSCR smokeboxes and chimneys were retained, together with the wooden brake blocks.

Repainted in LSWR livery as No. 734, and with Westinghouse brake pumps removed, the former No. 646 proceeded west for use at Lyme Regis. With coal rails now fitted, the 'Terrier' is lending a hand piloting at Exeter Queen Street.
*L&GRP collection, courtesy of David and Charles*

LWSR No. 734 has now become Freshwater, Yarmouth and Newport Railway (FYNR), No. 2. Shortly before going to the Island the 'Terrier' received a Drummond boiler (with safety valves on the dome), and is seen at the FYNR's Newport station.

*Lens of Sutton*

On 30th June 1913 the last IWCR train worked on the Freshwater, Yarmouth and Newport Railway (FYNR), after two years of talks which saw the parties getting gradually further apart. This meant that the FYNR had to find its own locomotives and rolling stock. Two engines were offered by the IWCR to the FYNR, No. 4, a 2-4-0 Beyer Peacock tank of 1876 vintage, and No. 6 an 1890 Black Hawthorne 4-4-0 tank. Both of these engines were rejected because of their price and mechanical condition. The LBSCR offered an 'E1' 0-6-0 tank No. 688 for £970 and a 'Terrier' No. 637 for £725; both of these locomotives required extensive boiler repairs so they too were rejected. A Manning Wardle 'Q' class contractors loco No. 56 *Northolt* was bought from Pauling and Elliott on 4th June 1913, and on 1st July 1913 the FYNR hired 'Terrier' No. 734 from the LSWR for 15 shillings (75p) per day plus shipment costs, with an option to buy in the following spring for £900. At a date not known No. 734 arrived at St. Helens and was taken by road to Newport. No. 56 became FYNR No. 1 and No. 734 became FYNR No. 2. On 18th December 1913 an agreement was made to purchase No. 734, which was completed in March 1914 for £900, with payment over five years at 5% interest. No hire charges were levied for the period from July 1913 to March 1914.

The engines worked with their bunkers facing towards Freshwater and this was very unpopular with the locomotive crews. In January 1916 the locomotives went to Sandown via Merstone, thence to Ryde St. Johns and back to Newport via Ashey, working round a large triangle. The engines now faced Freshwater, the locomotive crews were happy, and historians could as a consequence date photographs before or after January 1916; the FYNR was charged £4.13.8 for this excursion. No. 2 was painted in LSWR colours until February 1917. Following the final payment to the LSWR the locomotive was painted bright green lined in black and white, with scarlet coupling rods and lettered 'FYN' on the side tanks and '2' on the coal bunker side. During ten years that this 'Terrier' was owned by the FYNR routine repairs and general maintainnance were carried out by fitters from J.S. White and Company of Cowes. Normally this work was done on a Sunday during the summer months. If heavy boiler work was required the locomotive went to the IWR shops at Ryde, the IWCR charging £3 per trip (£6 return) over their metals. In April 1918 the FYNR asked the IWCR if they would overhaul No. 2, but they refused. Relations between the IWCR and the FYNR remained frosty. Recently a lady visiting the Isle of Wight Steam Railway said that No. 2 used to pull the trains that she travelled on to school in FYNR days. When it broke down, which was quite often, she and her friends used to pick the wild flowers that grew along the railway bank, much to the annoyance of the guard.

On becoming Southern Railway property, No. 2 became No. W2 in lined green livery, and received the usual extended bunker.

*Lens of Sutton*

For financial reasons the FYNR did not amalgamate on 1st January 1923 like other Island railways. The Southern Railway had offered £50,000 but the FYNR required £70,000, pointing out the potential of the Solent Tunnel (this project had been talked about for some years). The Southern took this into account and raised its offer to £60,000. When the FYNR refused the dispute went to an amalgamation tribunal, which considered £50,000 quite adequate. The FYNR was compulsorily absorbed into the Southern Railway on 1st September 1923 and so their 'Terrier' No. 2 joined the four others on the Island. In March 1924 its bunker was enlarged conforming to the pattern of the ex IWCR 'Terriers', the Westinghouse pump and brake gear was replaced after 21 year's absence and it was painted Maunsell green and its number changed from 2 to W2. No. W2 returned to traffic working the Freshwater branch again, with No. 10 to keep it company. At the next heavy overhaul in January 1927, steam heating equipment was fitted, together with motor train equip-

ment so that push-pull operation was possible. In October 1928 No. W2 was named *Freshwater*, the nameplates being fitted to the side tanks about half way down, with the word 'SOUTHERN' above and the number '2' below. This arrangement lasted until November 1929 when the nameplates were lowered to about two thirds of the way down the side tanks (centre line of name plate 14″ from the footplate) and the number '2', with the 'W' prefix above it, was put on the coal bunker side.

After general repairs at Ryde Works the old IWR Beyer Peacock 2-4-0 tank *Wroxall* started to work the Freshwater line in April 1931. The 'Terriers' which had worked the line for the past eight years, covering about a 150 miles a day, were finding the heavy holiday traffic hard work. *Wroxall* was later joined by another IWR 2-4-0 tank *Ryde*. When these locomotives were withdrawn in 1933 the LSWR 'O2' class locomotives were able to work the line because by then the whole line had been relaid and the viaducts strengthened.

*Above:* No. W2 was named *Freshwater* in October 1928. On the familiar ground of the Freshwater line, the 'Terrier' passes the old FYNR Newport station on 9th November 1928.
*H.C. Casserley*

*Right:* The rather congested appearance of the tank side was relieved by moving the number to the bunker side. In its last days as an 'AI', *Freshwater* is seen at Newport around 1930.
*O.J. Morris/Lens of Sutton*

Summer 1932. This 'Terrier' has now become 'AIX' No. W8 *Freshwater*, with a Drummond chimney, which is the condition in which it is restored. The classic picture of the newly rebuilt locomotive.

*O.J. Morris/Lens of Sutton*

No. W8 entering Newport with wagons loaded with chalk from Shide Quarry in June 1936.

*Lens of Sutton*

In January 1932 *Freshwater's* 1912 Drummond boiler was found to have a defective firebox, and rather than try to repair a non-standard boiler it was decided to rebuild her at Ryde works into an 'A1X' using new boiler No. 1226. The locomotive was fitted with a hooter, and a Drummond chimney, and like all Island 'A1X' rebuilds she retained the sandbox splashers. At the same time the loco was renumbered W8. Returning to traffic on 18th April 1932, No. W8 suffered initially from hot axle boxes and leaking boiler tubes, and seems to have spent most of the summer of 1932 in or around Newport yard getting photographed. When the faults were cured No. W8 worked all the usual branches including Bembridge and the Shide Quarry cement trains, though it normally worked the Merstone to Ventnor West motor trains. It was sometimes to be seen on the Freshwater line again, and August 1934 saw it shunting at Medina Wharf. Front steps were added, together with handrails at a date unknown; photographs show that it did run with a Drummond chimney and front steps fitted whilst working the Ventnor West Line. In December 1937 the boiler that had been on No. W11 (originally fitted to No.

663 and made in May 1913) was transferred to No. W8, which was repainted in Maunsell green, and its chimney replaced by an LBSCR Marsh chimney. In 1938 it was intended that No. W8 should return to the mainland; the nameplates were removed but for reasons unknown the transfer was cancelled and the 'Terrier' went back in to service with the nameplates refitted. During the war it was painted in unlined black and spent most of the time in store. With the war over No. W8 went into Ryde Works for repairs. It was decided to remove the Marsh chimney and replace it with a chimney that had been found in the works, which was later discovered to be the chimney that the engine had carried from new, which had been removed in 1932 when the Drummond chimney had been fitted. No. W8 returned to traffic on 13th August 1948, but on 13th April 1949 No. W8, together with No. W13, left the Island aboard the floating crane. They were unloaded at Southampton docks and arrived at Eastleigh works on 7th May. For the first time in 50 years the Island was without a 'Terrier'.

*Above:* No. W8 at Newport with a rake of ex-LCDR four wheeled coaches, set No. 489, in about 1938, now carrying a Marsh chimney, but no front steps.
*Lens of Sutton*

*Right:* Post war, with a copper capped chimney again, and with front steps added. No. W8 on the 5.27 pm from Merstone to Ventnor West on 18th April 1949.
*J.H. Aston*

*Left:* Back on the mainland, No. W8 became BR No. 32646, but did not receive lined black livery for quite a long time, and remained in this interim condition. Eastleigh, 19th August 1949, soon after return from the Island.

*A.F. Cork*

*Below:* For the major part of its time back on the mainland, No. 32646 worked on the Hayling Island branch. Here the 'Terrier' heads away from Havant in the later days, with spark arrester on chimney, coal rails on the bunker, and the second pattern of BR crest.

*Mike Esau*

On arrival at Eastleigh Works No. W8 received a light casual overhaul; it remained in unlined black but was now stripped of nameplates and numbered 32646, the number it would have carried if it had not gone to the LSWR and then the Isle of Wight. A new cast numberplate was fitted to the smokebox door (this plate is now in the Steam Railway's museum at Haven Street). The locomotive was fitted with a vacuum ejector on 6th August and her push-pull equipment removed a week later on 13th August. The newly renumbered 32646 left the shops at Eastleigh in August 1949 and went to Fratton shed for Hayling Island line duties. In December 1951 it returned to Brighton works for the first time in fifty years for repairs and a boiler change; its old boiler (No. 1014) was removed and was fitted to No. 32650 in May 1952. Boiler number 1170 was fitted to No.

32646, which was based at this time at Newhaven, returning to the Hayling Island line in August 1953. After a further spell at Newhaven from May 1954 No. 32646 it went back to Hayling Island line duties until February 1958, when it had a general overhaul at Brighton. It was the last locomotive to be overhauled at the Brighton works before they finally closed, and it acquired its present boiler No. BE1012, which was originally fitted to *Fenchurch* in April 1913, and it was painted in B.R. lined black. On 2nd November 1959 when Fratton shed closed No. 32646 was transferred to Eastleigh and remained working the Hayling Island line. Although an Eastleigh engine it did make trips to Brighton and Newhaven. With the closing of the Hayling Island line on 3rd November 1963 No. 32646 was withdrawn on 9th November 1963.

*Above:* No. 32646's first preservation home was at Droxford, on the Meon Valley line, where she was only steamed a few times; 19th December 1965.     *John Goss*

*Right:* In 1966 the 'Terrier' moved on, and was restored as No. 46 *Newington*, the largest public house sign in the South; 25th September 1966.

*John Goss*

The locomotive was first sold to the Hayling Terrier Fund, for £750. Unfortunately this Society was unsuccessful and No. 32646 was sold to Charles Ashby, of the Sadler Railcar Company, and moved to Droxford on part of the former Meon Valley line. This venture was also unsuccessful. The locomotive was then purchased by Brickwoods Brewery of Portsmouth, and on Friday 13th May 1966 it made its last run at 11 o'clock, with Sir Rupert Brickwood at the regulator, along the Meon Valley line, hauling a Southern Railway restaurant car. The author believes that some alcohol was consumed. The BBC, ITV and the press were in attendance (it would be nice to see some of this film); ninety years of work were finished. On Tuesday 17th May 1966 the 'Terrier' left Droxford and was shunted by diesel to Wickham, loaded on to a low loader and taken by road to Hayling Island to stand outside a public house called the *Hayling Billy*, the name given locally to the engine working the branch. The locomotive was painted in Stroudley livery with the original name *Newington*. The public house opened its doors on Wednesday 15th June 1966 at 6 pm and the opening ceremony was carried out by Drivers D. Sessions and G. McAskill who drove the engines which pulled the last train on the branch. The first pint was pulled by Guard F. Norris who had worked on the railway for 50 years, retiring in 1963 when the branch closed, and the first pint was drunk by Fireman M. Lee who fired on the last day. With these festivities over, the 'Terrier' then sat on its plinth outside of over a decade.

In 1975 the Isle of Wight Steam Railway made it known to the brewers Whitbread Wessex Limited (who had taken over Brickwoods) that it would be desirable to have this famous locomotive back in steam on the Isle of Wight. By 1979 other railways thought it would be desirable to see this locomotive on their lines, so Sir Peter Allen was asked to use his powers of diplomacy and persuasion. By Saturday 2nd June 1979 the good news arrived - Sir Peter had triumphed once again!

J. Hills of Botley were contracted to move the locomotive. Meanwhile Chris Whiting repainted *Newington* in two weekends and lo and behold! . . . . . No. W8 *Freshwater* stood outside the *Hayling Billy*. On Saturday 16th June, Len Pullinger and Ray Maxfield arrived on the scene to disconnect the motion to avoid another damaged cylinder (No. 11 had had thousands of pounds worth of damage done whilst being moved). Monday 18th was a fine day when the low loader arrived at Hayling Island. The Press and T.V. came to witness the event, photographs were taken, and by 4 o'clock the locomotive was ready to cross the Solent; but a dispute between Sealink and its employees delayed the crossing for a week. Monday 25th June 1979 saw *Freshwater* back on Island rails, and grateful thanks to Whitbreads were recorded for this generous gift.

Work started straight away to get *Freshwater* back in working order. On 19th October Mr. Graig, the boiler inspector, visited Haven Street and an on the spot meeting was held with him, Joe Snellgrove (the retired boilersmith from Ryde works), Len Pullinger and Ray Maxfield. *Freshwater's* boiler was not in such bad condition as some people feared. The front tube plate required welding to bring the plate back to its original thickness and new boiler tubes were fitted after a full internal inspection. The boiler was full of water and the firebox full of clinker from the 1966 steaming, 13 years 1 month and 1 day ago. The mechanical condition was very good, having been protected by a thick layer of oily grime, but the main and auxilliary reservoirs were found to be beyond repair and these were replaced. The chimney, which dated from 1876, was heavily rusted and so the Drummond chimney removed from No. 11 was fitted to *Freshwater*. She had carried a Drummond chimney identical to this one for five years. On 21st July 1980 the boiler inspector passed *Freshwater's* boiler with a 225 p.s.i. hydraulic pressure test.

In June 1979, as No. W8 *Freshwater*, the 'Terrier' returned once more to the Isle of Wight, and re-entered traffic two years later. Cleaned and ready for service on 26th June 1983, No. W8 poses with cleaners and firemen - Tim Spencer-Peet, Martyn Budd, Ian Corney, Gill Cato, Ally Beale, Toby Lindsey and Mike Salter. *Roger Macdonald*

Rumours had circulated that *Freshwater* had a non standard LSWR cylinder block of 13″ diameter, but this was found not to be true. It has a 14″ diameter cylinder block of LBSCR design, the same as No. 11. This standard 14″ cylinder block is thought to have been fitted in 1949 when it returned to the mainland. On a locomotive as old as *Freshwater* various numbers are usually found on the mechanical parts, and *Freshwater* is no exception. One of the valve spindles is stamped 734, the LSWR number, but most mysteriously two parts have been found marked 2646, a number which the engine never carried; there is no trace of anything marked 2 or 8. The boiler was steamed on 22nd August and again on 28th September 1980. Apart from one leaking tube end and some minor leaks and knocks everything went well. During the winter the coal bunker and the boiler cladding sheets were replaced. The cab roof required repairing and the small holes turned out to need large patches. Chris Whiting then took over to paint and line the locomotive once again.

On 21st June 1981 No. W8 *Freshwater* returned to traffic. Sir Peter Allen gave the principal speech, followed by Mr. McNab of Whitbread Wessex and Mr. Bray of Freshwater Parish Council. After the speeches *Freshwater* hauled a special train for members and invited guests at 12.45 pm, and then hauled the 1.30 pm normal scheduled train. *Freshwater* became the main work horse for the rest of the running season covering 887 miles with only one small breakdown on the Westinghouse pump. During the winter of 1981-82 further work was carried out to the frames, horn blocks and axleboxes; the name 'Monkbridge' was found stamped in the frames. No. W8 returned to traffic in June but coupling rod bushes were overheating, so careful measurements were made and the coupling rods were found to be 5/16″ too long. When they were rebushed at Eastleigh in 1962 an eccentric bush had been replaced by a concentric bush, hence the axlebox trou-

ble. After repairs *Freshwater* returned to service and ran 980 miles during 1982. The winter of 1982-83 saw minor routine work done, though a visit by the boiler inspector caused a last minute panic when he asked for some work to be done on the firehole door rivets in the firebox. *Freshwater* started hauling trains at Easter 1983, and continued as a very reliable engine through 1983, covering 1,177 miles. During 1983 at Haven Street a boiler washout wagon was built, and this, together with a water treatment programme, has helped with boiler maintenance. On 25th January 1984, the boiler inspector gave *Freshwater's* boiler a clean bill of health after a visual inspection.

In the spring of 1984 No. W8 was the only steam loco that was in a serviceable condition. It performed well although due to a year long miners' strike the only coal available contained a large amount of rock and slate. This resulted in a lot of fire cleaning. The saddle-tank *Invincible* was back in service on 21st June; after a few teething troubles she ran well, and the two little locomotives coped quite well during the summer show. On 29th September *Invincible* was taken out of service with loose rivets in its frame and brake gear. The rivets were tightened and replaced. No. W8's mileage for 1984 was 1097. During the winter of 1984/85 new piston rings were fitted to the cylinders; the old ones were worn out and had started to give trouble.

No. W8 was busy again in 1985, achieving its highest annual mileage yet (in preservation) of 1188. *Freshwater* was out of service from Spring to August in 1986, to allow major firebox repairs including building up of seams by welding, and remachining of eccentric straps. The mileage in 1986 was only 506.

Most of the time this loco carries the brunt of the traffic on the Isle of Wight Steam Railway, though it is less popular than the 'O2' *Calbourne*. The 'Terrier' regularly hauls trains of 4 bogie coaches of 130 tons gross weight up and down the line.

The restored No. W8 has been regularly at work since 1981, and is seen going about its business on the Isle of Wight Steam Railway.
*Colin Fairweather*

# No. W13 Carisbrooke

The five 'Terriers' described so far were all bought by one or other of the independent Island railway companies. We now come to the three 'Terriers' sent out to the Island by the Southern Railway.

The first of these three was a locomotive which entered service on 21st July 1880, and was the 44th 'Terrier' to be built; it was named *Wonersh* (after a village just outside Guildford) and was numbered 77. Initially shedded at Bramley, No. 77 worked the Horsham to Guildford line, together with No. 36 *Bramley*, and when Bramley shed closed the two locomotives were shedded at Guildford (LSWR), with maintenance being done at Horsham on a Sunday. In 1895 it was fitted with 14″ diameter cylinders and its condensing pipes were removed. At this time it was working the Midhurst line from Pulborough to Chichester, together with No. 42 *Tulsehill* and No. 82 *Boxhill*, but in 1905 No. 77 was put into store, along with 14 other 'Terriers'.

In 1907 Push-Pull and Railcars were in vogue. *Wonersh* was renumbered 677, stripped of its name and painted in Marsh umber brown livery; it was equipped with mechanically operated push-pull gear and its cylinders were sleeved down to 12″ diameter. No. 677 was then sent to work from Tunbridge Wells depot. The 'Terrier' workings of push-pull services were very successful; they were fast, reliable and economical. 1911 saw the start of reboilering of the 'Terriers'; this had first been suggested in 1906, but with so many 'Terriers' in store the subject had been dropped. In 1911, with the 'Terriers' working the Motor Train services and being so successful, the situation had changed. No. 677 was the first to be reboilered, having covered 925,078 miles, and thus became the first of the 'A1X' class. The cost was £898 and the change was completed in November 1911 (Boiler No. 934). No. 677 returned to Tunbridge Wells, working services that took it to Oxted, East Grinstead, Three Bridges, Horsham, and Haywards Heath. Its daily mileage would have been about 230 miles, with a very respectable weekly figure of 1,400 miles; in LBSCR days No. 677 was a consistently high mileage 'Terrier'. Speeds of over 60 mph were common on a good track, and the 'Terriers' were quite stable at that speed. No. 677's coal consumption at this time was 16.4 lb per mile, which was also very good. The Tunbridge Wells shed 'Terrier' stud in March 1912 was 'A1' 667, 'A1X' 673, 'A1X' 677 and 'A1' 682, but by December 1916 No. 673 had been transferred to Horsham, followed by No. 677, to work the Midhurst - Chichester line. By the end of 1922 No. 677 had clocked up 1,230,531 miles, the highest Terrier mileage at this point. However in September 1925 No. 677 was taken out of service and put into store in the paint shop at Preston Park (just north of Brighton).

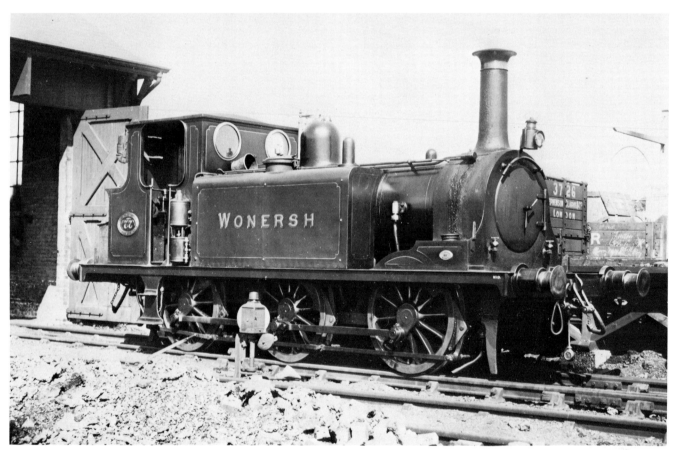

The 'Terrier' that became No. W13 began as LBSCR No. 77 *Wonersh* (later No. 677). This engine was based at Midhurst for some years, and this is where it is seen here, somewhere around 1900.
*Lens of Sutton*

*Right:* By the time No. 677 went to the Isle of Wight as No. W3 in 1927, some changes had been made. The engine had been the first conversion to 'AIX', and an extended bunker had been fitted. Seen at Newport around 1928.

*Lens of Sutton*

*Below:* The 'new boy' at work; No. W3 on the Freshwater branch in the summer of 1927.

*Lens of Sutton*

With No. W9 on the Isle of Wight showing signs of age, No. 677 was not broken up as planned, but was sent in December 1926 to Brighton Works for repairs, emerging in February 1927. Boiler feed pumps were removed and injectors fitted, the coal bunker was extended in the Isle of Wight style, the loco was painted in Maunsell green and, with 'SOUTHERN' and 'W3' painted on the side tanks, it was shipped to the Island in May 1927. It took over No. W9's duties and was seen working the Freshwater line in 1927; it was equipped for push-pull motor train operation at Ryde Works. In the autumn of 1928 it was allocated the name *Carisbrooke*, and carried the nameplates about two thirds of the way down the side tanks under the word 'SOUTHERN', whilst the number 'W3' was painted on the coal bunker. The name plates were fitted in 1929.

In 1930 it was transferred from Newport to Ryde Shed, fitted with a hooter and worked the Bembridge branch; its number was changed to W13 in April 1932. As it retained 12″ cylinders, it did not receive a Drummond chimney, and retained the copper-capped chimney whilst on the Island; hence it was known as "Coffee Pot" by the locals. A boiler change took place in May 1932; the new boiler was No. 1128 (built in May 1920). In about 1935 front steps were fitted, together with vertical hand rails on the front of the side tanks, to help the locomotive crew to reach the top half of the locomotive when it was not in a station.

No. W13 worked the Bembridge branch during the winter of 1935-36 with the LCDR 4 wheeled Push-Pull set No. 484. This set normally worked on the Ventnor West line, but was transferred to the Bembridge branch whilst the 16′ 5″ Turntable at Bembridge was replaced by a new 25′ 0″ diameter turntable which enabled LSWR 'O2' Class Locomotives to be used on the branch.

No. W3 was named *Carisbrooke* in 1929 and renumbered W13 in 1932. This 'Terrier' was a regular on the Bembridge branch in the early 1930s, and is seen running into Brading, from the branch, during this period.

*Lens of Sutton*

Ready to leave Brading for Bembridge, again in the early 1930s. This 'Terrier' did not receive a Drummond chimney.

*Lens of Sutton*

In about 1935 No. W13 was fitted with front steps, and grab handles on the tank fronts. Very smartly turned out in this condition, the locomotive sits at Newport in the late 1930s.

*Lens of Sutton*

No. W13 was the only Island 'Terrier' to receive malachite green livery, and retained it for some years on the mainland. This is the locomotive's final Island condition.
*J.H. Aston*

Uniformity finally prevailed, and the former No. W13, as BR No. 32677, ran its final years in lined black livery, but retained the copper capped chimney to the end.
*Lens of Sutton*

With the departure of 'Terriers' Nos. 10, 12, 14 and the second No. 9 from the Island in 1936, the remaining duties - the Ventnor West line, shunting at Medina Wharf, working the chalk trains from Pan Lane Pit (near Shide) to the cement mills (near Mill Hill), general piloting and shunting duties - were shared out between the three remaining 'Terriers'; this continued until 1947. During the war No. W13 was seen on piloting duties at Newport, and at the end of the war in 1945, it was painted in malachite green and fully lined out, making a fine sight that was widely commented on. With the departure of No. W11 to the mainland in 1947, Nos. W8 and W13 shared the working of the Ventnor West line. 1948 saw No. W13 working the branch whilst No. W8 was repaired; as the branch did not run trains on a Sunday, boiler washouts and small repairs were done then. On 17th and 24th of September 1948 'O2' class No. 27 *Merstone* worked

the branch; for an 'O2' to work this branch was rare at this time, but was a foretaste of things to come.

On 13th April 1949 No. W13, along with No. W8, left the Island, returning to Eastleigh on 7th May 1949. It was stored at the back of the running shed for several weeks, and it was then given a light casual repair and renumbered 32677, returning to traffic on the Hayling Island line. In September 1952 it was painted in BR lined black at Brighton Works, 6″ high numerals being used, and it returned to the Hayling Island line to join Nos. 32655 (former *Stepney*) 32661 and 32646 (former W8). After a final general repair in 1957, No. 32677 was withdrawn in September 1959. A final mileage figure of 1,301,612 was quoted, but this is definitely wrong, and the true figure probably exceeded 1,500,000 miles. This fine 'Terrier' was cut up at Eastleigh at the end of April 1960, still carrying a copper-capped chimney.

# No. W14 Bembridge

The last two Island 'Terriers' form a special category of their own. They had by far the shortest careers on the Island, and both of them are preserved, but neither is preserved on the Island. The first of these two was the second of the three 'Terriers' sent to the Island by the Southern.

It was the 45th 'Terrier' to be built, leaving the erecting shops on 23rd July 1880. Numbered 78 and originally named *Knowle* (after a small village just south of Sevenoaks in Kent), it was shedded at New Cross along with other 'Terriers' to work the East London Line services. In the mid eighties No. 78 moved to Tunbridge Wells shed, New Cross Shed having been supplied with more powerful 'D1' class 0-4-2 tanks. 1894 saw the removal of the condensing pipes and the fitting of new 14″ diameter cylinders, replacing the 13″ ones carried from new. In the nineties *Knowle* moved on to Portsmouth to work the Hayling Island Line and the East Southsea Branch together with Nos. 43 *Gipsy Hill*, 48 *Leadenhall* and 71 *Wapping*.

In 1907 No. 78 was fitted with Marsh's mechanical push-pull equipment, the cylinders were sleeved down to 12″ diameter, and to reduce running costs still further the steam condensing pipes were replaced. The locomotive was renumbered 678, lost its name, and was painted in the new Marsh livery of the LBSCR. In November 1911 No. 678 received an 'A1X' Boiler (No. BE 935) becoming the second conversion to 'A1X', and leaving the works only seven days after the first, No. 677. Mileage stood at 763,933. On leaving Brighton works No. 678 went at Horsham shed, joining No. 659 to work the Bognor trains. Marsh's mechanical push-pull system worked well providing it was properly maintained, but in 1912 the Brighton trains were converted to the Westinghouse compressed air system. 1916 saw No. 678 shedded at Littlehampton along with No. 662, and in November 1918 it moved to the London area, being shedded at West Croydon. At the Grouping of the railways at the end of 1922 it was back at Horsham, having covered a total of 949,056 miles.

No. 678 continued in service until September 1925 when its services were no longer required and it was put into store at Preston Park (just north of Brighton) paint shop and remained there until early 1929. The Isle of Wight required another 'Terrier' and No. 678 went into Brighton Works to be made ready for the Island. It was completely overhauled, its boiler going to Terrier No. E735 (the ex LSWR 735) and it received boiler No. 965 (formerly 951), taken from Terrier No. B661. Injectors were fitted, feed pumps were removed, and it was fitted with an IOW extended coal bunker and was repainted in the Island style leaving a space for nameplates. Records show that new 14″ diameter cylinders were fitted on 28th February 1929 at Brighton, and the locomotive was renumbered W4 and shipped to the Island in May 1929. The name *Bembridge* was allocated to No. 8, the 1896 2-4-0 Beyer Peacock tank, but this loco was scrapped before receiving the bronze nameplates specially cast at Eastleigh, so the name was given to No. W4 instead. Push-pull train operating equipment was fitted on arrival on the Island and No. W4 was shedded at Ryde to work the Bembridge branch for a short while, but was then transferred to Newport for Freshwater line duties.

*Bembridge*, like *Carisbrooke*, had a number change - rather a rare event on the Island; in 1932 it was renumbered W14. This was done so that the four new arrivals, the Brighton 0-6-0 'E1' Class tank locomotives, could be numbered W1 to W4. *Bembridge* seems to have eluded most of the photographers whilst on the Island - not many photographs exist of this engine. With the relaying of track and the strengthening of viaducts the LSWR 'O2' locomotives could work most of the lines including the Bembridge branch and the Freshwater line. No. W14 was one of the four Terriers returned to the mainland in May 1936, and the name was transferred to the newly arrived 'O2' class No. W33.

No. 78 *Knowle*, which later became No. W14, in about 1900.                    *Lens of Sutton*

'Terrier' in waiting. No. 78 has become 'A1X' No. 678, with condensing pipes and coal rails, and is in store at Preston Park. No. 678's companion is ex-SECR No. 751, and this is probably about 1928, towards the end of the period of store.

*Lens of Sutton*

No. W14 was condemned in December 1936 but was reprieved before scrapping; the loco was taken into Eastleigh Works for a general overhaul, when it was renumbered 2678 and received boiler No. BE 967, built new in 1912 and carried by No. 653 from new until 1935 (this boiler is now on No. 11 *Newport*). Returning to traffic in July 1937 its new shed was Fratton and its new place of work the Hayling Island line once again. But March 1938 saw No. 2678 heading north for Guildford, where it was given trials as shed pilot, but was found unsuitable and returned to Fratton. The next trip, in February 1940, was to the Kent and East Sussex Railway (which was still under private ownership); the loco was shedded on loan at Rolvenden, remaining there until after the line became part of British Railways. While working on the K & ESR No. 2678 had general repairs at Ashford, and at one such repair, between May and

August 1948, it was given to British Railways number 32678. This 'Terrier' had a very long stay on the Kent & East Sussex line, and the most serious incident was when, on 29th March 1949, it was derailed near Wittersham Road, coming to rest on its right hand side in swampy ground. It was rescued and taken to Brighton Works for repair and repainting, receiving the new British Railways lined black livery. No. 32678 then returned to the Kent & East Sussex line and continued to work there until 2nd June 1958, when it returned to Hayling Island duties once again, being shedded at Fratton. General repairs and a boiler change were carried out in May 1953, and at the final general overhaul in September 1959 the present boiler No. 1128 was fitted and the loco was repainted. When Fratton shed closed No. 32678 was moved at Eastleigh, with all the other Hayling Island 'Terriers' but returned to the Kent & East Sussex Railway to make three

'Terrier' transformed! With Marsh chimney and extended bunker, and without condensing pipes. This shot of No. W4 *Bembridge* is at Newport in about 1930.

*Lens of Sutton*

*Above:* No. W4 was renumbered W14 in 1932, and received a Drummond chimney. Here the locomotive is at work on the Freshwater line, crossing the tressle river bridge just outside Newport on 24th July 1935.   *S.W. Baker*

*Right:* Back to the mainland, after only seven years on the Island, No. W14 at Eastleigh in 1936. The wooden blocks fitted for lifting are still in place.

*Lens of Sutton*

Unlike Nos. W10 and W12, return to the mainland was not the end of the road for No. W14. Overhauled and returned to service as No. 2678, it is seen in Fratton shed on 28th August 1938.

*S.W. Baker*

farewell runs in 1961. In May 1963 it was transferred to Brighton and took up duties at the West Quay in Newhaven, and in June 1963 it was back at Brighton on coal shed piloting duties. It was the last 'Terrier' on duty at Newhaven before the old Harbour lines, long the haunts of *Fenchurch*, finally closed, and was the last 'Terrier' to leave Brighton. On 5th October 1963, it was sent to Eastleigh and was withdrawn, having covered a total of 1,389,447 Miles.

No. 32678 was one of the three 'Terriers' bought by Billy Butlin for display at his holiday camps, and was painted in a form of Stroudley livery and sent to the Minehead camp in July 1964. The 'Terrier' remained on display there until in April 1975 it was moved to the nearby West Somerset Railway and later sold to a

group of the railway's supporters and housed in a barn. By early 1983 the project of restoring this locomotive (now dismantled) had become too expensive for the group and they offered the locomotive to the Bluebell Railway. Keith Sturt, Jack Owen and Ray Bellingham went down to Somerset to inspect it but decided that there was too much work required to get it back into running order, the boiler requiring extensive attention.

Instead the 'Terrier' was bought by a director of Resco Railways, and was taken, in dismantled form, in April 1983 to Resco premises at Woolwich, where some restoration work was done. Then, in 1988, the parts of the dismantled locomotive were moved to the Kent & East Sussex Railway at Rolvenden, where it is planned that the restoration will be completed.

*Above:* After only about 2½ years at Fratton, No. 2678 was sent to work on the Kent & East Sussex Railway, and stayed there for 18 years. So this is a typical scene from the 'Terriers' life, at Robertsbridge on 16th July 1947.
*The late George Kerley*

*Right:* Later in its K&ESR stay, as BR No. 32678, the locomotive assumed the standard latter day 'Terrier' appearance. Shortly after a general overhaul, and still looking very smart, No. 32678 is at Ashford on 12th August 1953. *J.H. Aston*

# No. W9 Fishbourne

With the final Island 'Terrier' we have come full circle, as it carried the same number as the first 'Terrier' on the Island, but it only had a brief six year connection with the Island. It was the 27th 'Terrier' completed, leaving the erecting shops on 14th December 1876, numbered 50 and named *Whitechapel*. It joined other 'Terriers' at New Cross shed, working services on the East London line and to Croydon. In 1893 its 13″ cylinders were replaced by standard 14″ ones, and steam condensing pipes were removed, which was common, 41 of 50 'Terriers' receiving this modification.

In 1901 No. 50's number was changed to 650, but towards the end of 1905 it was put in store along with 14 other 'Terriers'. 1907 saw a reprieve when it was taken out of store and fitted with Marsh push-pull equipment along with 21 other 'Terriers'. In common with these other 'Terriers', its cylinders were sleeved down to 12″ dia, steam condensing pipes were refitted to the side tanks, and it was repainted in the new LBSCR Marsh livery. Although all 'Terriers' lost their names on their side tanks, railway personnel continued to refer to them by name rather than number. During March 1912 No. 650 was at Fratton with Nos. 643 and 679 working the Hayling Island line, and in July 1913 the push-pull equipment was changed to the Westinghouse compressed air system. In December 1916 No. 650 was at Bognor along with No. 680, working in the mid Sussex area. In May 1920, after covering 867,984 miles, it was reboiled to the usual mainland 'A1X' specification at a cost of £1,195; the boiler number was 1128. When the LBSCR ceased to exist at the end of 1922 No. 650 had covered 951,269 miles and was shedded at Portsmouth. In 1926 its number was changed to B650.

In May 1930 the Isle of Wight required another 'Terrier' for the summer season, and No. B650 was chosen. It was completely overhauled at Brighton, and fitted with an Isle of Wight coal bunker; the cylinders were checked on 6th May and measured 12 1/16″ diameter. On the trial run the boiler was leaking badly, so the boiler which had just been taken from No. B662, boiler No. 1008 (former No. 986) built in October 1912, was hastily fitted. The locomotive was renumbered W9 and was painted in the Isle of Wight style and sent to Eastleigh where it was fitted with motor train working equipment (though this equipment may have been fitted at Ryde works). The second No.

W9 crossed the Solent in late May 1930, and on arrival it was named *Fishbourne* (a village near Wootton). The new No. W9's duties were working the Bembridge branch, alternating with No. W3, the branch being worked on the 'one engine in steam' system. When the new 25 foot diameter turntable was installed, in the winter of 1935/36, replacing the old 16 foot 5 inch diameter table, LSWR 'O2' class locomotives could work the branch. So the second No. W9 became surplus to requirements and returned to the mainland in May 1936, having covered a total of 1,069,877 miles.

The displaced locomotive was stored at Eastleigh until April 1937 when it was transferred to departmental stock; renumbered 515S it became one of the Lancing Carriage Works pilots, a quiet life with few incidents. August 1946 saw it converted to oil burning, but this system proved very troublesome, and although many modifications were made it was decided to return the locomotive to coal burning as before. In February 1952 it had a general overhaul and boiler change, receiving boiler BE 1014 (from No. W8). The loco was painted in unlined black with the words "C & W Lancing Works" on the side tanks and its BR number DS 515 on the coal bunker side. But the following year this 'Terrier's' quiet life was ended, and it returned to ordinary running stock.

In August 1953 'Terrier' No. 32659 was transferred to departmental stock, renumbered DS 681 and painted in unlined black. It went to take up duties at Lancing Works on 6th November 1953. In exchange, No. DS515 went into Brighton Works and was painted lined black and renumbered 32650, taking its correct number in the 'Terrier' sequence. The reason for this change of locomotives was two fold:-

a) 32650, being an ex-Island engine, had a large coal bunker which was favoured on the Hayling Island line.
b) 32560 was in much better condition than 32659.

In February 1957 No. 32650 had general repairs at Brighton together with a boiler change, and again in March 1963 at Eastleigh. It continued throughout to work on Hayling Island line duties where it remained until the line closed in November 1963.

The final Island 'Terrier' was originally No. 50 *Whitechapel*, later renumbered 650; the brass number plates have been removed and the new number painted on.

*Lens of Sutton*

*Right:* Unlike the other two 'Terriers' sent to the Island by the Southern, SR No. B650 was active in the 1920s on the mainland. In lined green livery, No. B650 is carriage piloting at Brighton.
*Lens of Sutton*

*Below:* The usual transformation. No. B650 went to the Island as No. W9 *Fishbourne* in 1930, and had probably only just arrived when this photograph was posed, at Newport.
*O.J. Morris/Lens of Sutton*

On the last day of regular services (Saturday 2nd November 1963) the trains were strengthened to three coaches and after the 2.20 pm from Havant a special service operated at 30 minute intervals. This required two trains and three locomotives, the engines used being Nos. 32650, 32662 and 32670; the last train from Havant was the 8.39 pm which left 20 minutes late, hauled by No. 32662. The last public train, the 9 pm from Hayling Island, consisted of 6 coaches hauled by No. 32650 and pushed by No. 32662. The train left 30 minutes late and arrived at Havant at 9.50 pm. On Sunday 3rd November 1963 a farewell tour was arranged by the Locomotive Club of Great Britain and this train was hauled by Nos. 32636 and 32670. No. 32650 was put into store at Eastleigh having covered 1,271,019 miles.

Early in 1964 the then Borough of Sutton and Cheam decided to purchase 'Terrier' No. 32661, formerly No. 61 *Sutton*, which was withdrawn in April 1963, but unfortunately this had been broken up in September 1963. The Borough decided that No. 32650 would be an acceptable substitute and went ahead and purchased it, planning to display the 'Terrier' in the new Civic Centre and to acknowledge the part played by the railways in developing the Sutton area. As the new Civic Centre was still some way off, the Borough accepted an offer from the Kent & East Sussex Railway to house and restore the 'Terrier' to working order, to carry the name *Sutton* on the side tanks. British Railways agreed to deliver No. 32650 to Robertsbridge (the K & ESR link with BR) for £17, and it arrived there on 19th September 1964.

Following delivery to Robertsbridge in September 1964, it remained there until Whitsun 1966 when it was used to haul carriage stock to Rolvenden. It remained at Rolvenden where it was officially named *Sutton*. During 1968/9 it was overhauled and provided with new dome cast locally at Rye Foundry. It was given the running number 50 and painted in the then standard light green livery of the K & ESR Society. The name was painted on the side tanks in yellow with a Borough of Sutton transfer crest above (as used on municipal vehicles). It was steamed regularly from 1969 to 1972. It was then withdrawn for attention which included work on cylinders, valves, motion, and firebox. The running number was changed to 10, and same green livery was retained.

Most of *Fishbourne's* time on the Island was spent on the Bembridge branch and like No. W13, this 'Terrier' did not receive a Drummond chimney. No. W9 is at Bembridge on a branch working on 17th July 1932.
*F.M. Butterfield/R.C. Riley collection*

In the spring of 1973 the cylinders and motion were reassembled, following work on the axle journals. The piston rods were reground and replated to increase the life of the cylinder packing, this work being done by Norman Payne, an ex BR Bricklayers Arms (a shed off the Old Kent Road in South East London) boilermaker and Bob Forsythe, a BR Cricklewood (a shed in North West London on LMSR) employee. Repairs were also carried out to the boiler, and the locomotive was back in service for Christmas 1973.

During 1974 *Sutton* worked well and covered 278 miles. On one particular day it worked three return trips from Tenterden to Rolvenden plus light engine trips and some light shunting, with a total day's consumption of coal of only 10 cwt. At the end of the season work was carried out on the Westinghouse pump, all valves and reservoirs, and the pipework was completely replaced. The smokebox and side tanks were given some new plate work, and the boiler was retubed; the engine was repainted by David Dine and Cathy Artlett, receiving two undercoats and two finishing coats and also receiving new nameplates made by Mike Please. Although it was hoped to have the 'Terrier' back in service in November 1974, it was December 1975 when it re-entered service. *Sutton* worked through 1976, celebrating its one hundredth birthday, and in 1977, when it ran 1,216 miles and spent some 491 hours in steam. In 1978 it was withdrawn for boiler inspection, but passed the tests and returned to traffic in August 1978 after routine boiler repairs. Steam heating equipment was fitted for the Christmas 1978 period working (Santa Specials).

*Sutton* started the 1979 season but was withdrawn for a boiler hydraulic test at the end of July. The boiler inspector allowed the engine to continue working to the end of the year,

but it was withdrawn on 1st February 1980 for extensive repairs. In 1981 six firms tendered for the repair work on the boiler; there was talk of a new firebox and even possibly a completely new boiler. The boiler was lifted out of the frames early in 1982. The boiler inspector decided that it would require a new firebox, smokebox, a retube and a considerable number of new rivets and stays. The boiler was sent to Resco (Railway) Ltd on 1st June 1982, and there it was repaired under the direction of Norman Payne, who was then an employee of Resco's. The inner copper firebox was removed, repaired and refitted, together with 258 new stays. The boiler was sent to Resco (Railways) Ltd on 1st June 1983 works of the KESR on 4th November 1983. Whilst the boiler was away, the engine was overhauled mechanically, this part of the job turning out to be much bigger than originally thought. The boiler was returned to the frames in the spring of 1984, a new blast pipe was fitted and some work was carried out on the cab and bunker. No. 10 returned to service on 28th May 1984. After an unveiling ceremony of a new brass name plate, by the Mayor of Sutton, Councillor Joyce K.M. Bowley, *Sutton* hauled the 12.10 train. The overhaul had cost £15,000.

*Sutton* remained in service after this, but had to be withdrawn with a cracked cylinder. To avoid having to cast a new cylinder block, it was decided to use metal surgery to repair this crack. The first attempt was unsuccessful, but the second attempt worked, and *Sutton* was able to return to service on 10th April 1988. The locomotive had been repainted in Southern Railway lined green as No. 10 *Sutton*, and so now appears to be an Island 'Terrier' once more. But of course it was really No. 9 when on the Island, and the real Isle of Wight No. 10 is long since gone - which is perhaps a bit confusing!

*Right:* On return to the mainland in 1936, No. W9 was dumped at Eastleigh, but was sent the next year to work at Lancing Carriage Works, as departmental No. 515S. After the war the locomotive was briefly fitted for oil burning, as seen here on 1st September 1946.

*O.J. Morris/Lens of Sutton*

*Above:* On return to running stock in 1953 as BR No. No. 32650, this 'Terrier' was sent to work on the Hayling Island branch. It is seen crossing Langstone Bridge in the last days of the island branch line.

*John Goss*

*Right:* Though now preserved and active, this 'Terrier' has not returned to the Island. No. 32650, now owned by the Borough of Sutton, resides at the Kent & East Sussex Railway as their No. 10 *Sutton*, where it ran for several years in a light green lined livery.

*Author*

# Appendix I

## Dimensions as built

Some details of the 'Terriers' as built are given below:

| | |
|---|---|
| Cylinders (2) | 13″ diam × 20″ stroke |
| Wheels | 3′ 11″ diam, later 4′ 0″ |
| Wheelbase | 6′ 0″ + 6′ 0″ |
| Overall length | 26′ 0½″ |
| Overall height | 11′ 3″ |
| Overall width | 7′ 2″ |
| Boiler diameter | 3′ 6″ |
| Boiler length | 7′ 10″ |
| Firebox length | 4′ 1″ |

Heating surfaces:

| | |
|---|---|
| Tubes 125 × 1¾″ diam = | 473 sq ft |
| Firebox | 55 sq ft |
| Total | 528 sq ft |

| | |
|---|---|
| Grate area | 10.3 sq ft |
| Boiler pressure | 140 p.s.i. |
| Weight in working order | 24 tons 12 cwt – equally divided |
| Fully laden weight | 26 tons 17 cwt |
| Side tank capacity | 500 gallons |
| Coal bunker capacity | 10 cwt |

C.J. Binnie

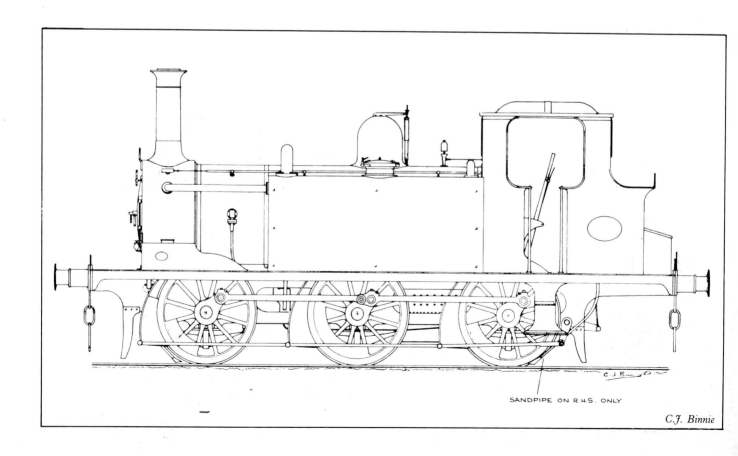

SANDPIPE ON R.H.S. ONLY

*C.J. Binnie*

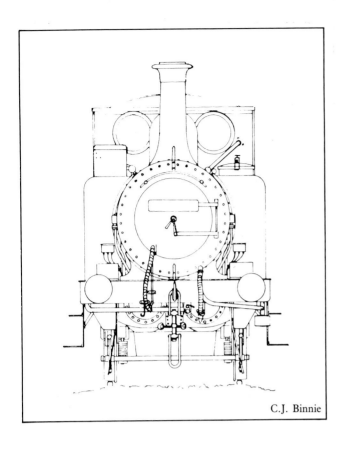

C.J. Binnie

# Appendix II

## Latter day dimensions

The dimensions of an 'A1X' class tank engine, as given on the BR engine record cards of the survivors, are:

2 cylinders, 14″ bore × 20″ stroke, 150 lbs/sq in boiler pressure, 4′ 0″ diameter driving wheels.

$$\text{Tractive effort} = \frac{14 \times 14 \times 20 \times 150 \times 0.85}{48}$$
$$= 10,412 \text{ lbs}$$

Slide valves, Stephenson link motion, lever reversing gear

| | |
|---|---|
| Engine wheelbase | = 12′ 0″ |
| Overall length | = 26′ 0½″ |
| Overall height | = 11′ 0¾″ |
| Radius of minimum negotiable curve | = 3.74 chains |
| Total weight in working order | = 28 tons 5 cwt |
| Grate area | = 10.0 sq ft |
| 119 boiler tubes of 1¾″ | |
| Heating surface | = 488.72 sq ft |

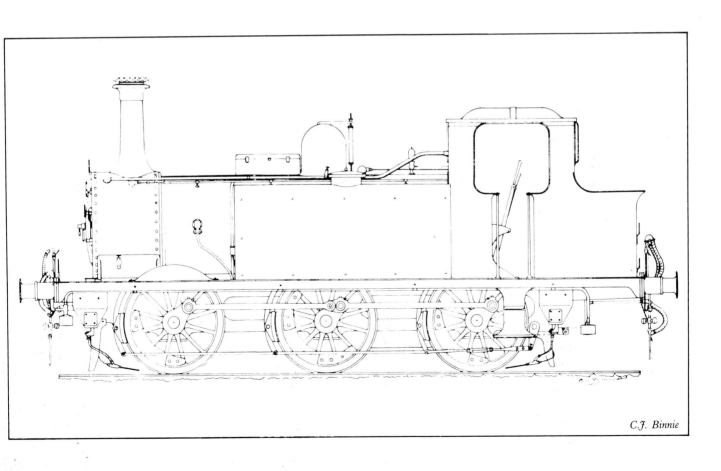

C.J. Binnie

# Appendix III

## Summary of the Island Terriers

Five Terriers were owned by the independent Island railway companies, as follows:

| LBSCR No. | Name | Service Date | To IoW | IoW Co. | No. | A1X Date | Southern No. | Name | To Mainland | Disposal |
|---|---|---|---|---|---|---|---|---|---|---|
| 75 | **Blackwall** | 11/72 | 3/99 | IWCR | 9 | – | W9 | – | – | Withdrawn 4/26 |
| 69 | **Peckham** | 7/74 | 4/00 | IWCR | 10 | 4/30 | W10 | **Cowes** | 5/36 | Cut up 3/49 |
| 40 | **Brighton** | 3/78 | 1/02 | IWCR | 11 | 7/18 | W11 | **Newport** | 2/47 | Preserved |
| 84 | **Crowborough** | 9/80 | 11/03 | IWCR | 12 | 7/16 | W12 | **Ventnor** | 5/36 | Cut up 4/49 |
| 46 | **Newington** | 1/77 | 6/13 | FYNR | 2 | 4/32 | W2,W8 | **Freshwater** | 4/49 | Preserved |

Three further Terriers were sent to the Island by the Southern Railway, as follows:

| LBSCR No. | Name | Service Date | A1X Date | To IoW | IoW No. | Name | To Mainland | Disposal |
|---|---|---|---|---|---|---|---|---|
| 77 | **Wonersh** | 7/80 | 11/11 | 5/27 | W3,W13 | **Carisbrooke** | 4/49 | Cut up 4/60 |
| 78 | **Knowle** | 7/80 | 11/11 | 5/29 | W4,W14 | **Bembridge** | 5/36 | Preserved |
| 50 | **Whitechapel** | 12/76 | 5/20 | 5/30 | W9 | **Fishbourne** | 5/36 | Preserved |

The durations these locomotives stayed on the Island were:

| Loco | | To Island | From Island | Duration |
|---|---|---|---|---|
| W9 | (the first) | March 1899 | April 1926 | 27 years 1 month |
| W10 | **Cowes** | April 1900 | May 1936 | 36 years 1 month |
| W11 | **Newport** | January 1902 | February 1947 | 45 years 1 month |
| W12 | **Ventnor** | November 1903 | May 1936 | 32 years 6 months |
| W8 | **Freshwater** | June 1913 | April 1949 | 35 years 10 months |
| W13 | **Carisbrooke** | May 1927 | April 1949 | 21 years 11 months |
| W14 | **Bembridge** | May 1929 | May 1936 | 7 years 0 months |
| W9 | **Fishbourne** | May 1930 | May 1936 | 6 years 0 months |

# Appendix IV

## A1X Boilers on the Isle of Wight

Only two 'A1X' boilers went to the Isle of Wight in pre-Grouping days:

No. 1094 – new on IWCR No. 12 (7/16), to No. W10 (4/30); back to mainland on No. W10 (5/36); cut up 1949

No. 1111 – new on IWCR No. 11 (7/18), to No. W12 (12/29); back to mainland on No. W12 (5/36); cut up 1949

Further boilers were sent to the Island in SR times. Identification of these is somewhat confused as several were given new numbers by Eastleigh Works, as their Brighton Works numbers were already carried by existing Eastleigh boilers.

No. 1014 – new on No. 663 (5/13); to IoW as spare and fitted to No. W11 (12/27), to No. W8 (12/37); back to mainland on No. W8 in 1949; now preserved on *Fenchurch*

No. 186 (Brighton No. 934) – new on No. 677 (11/11); to IoW on No. W3 (ex 677) (3/27), to No. W11 (7/33); back to mainland as spare approx 1947; cut up approx 1961.

No. 965 (Brighton No. 951) – new on No. 661 (1/12); to IoW on No. W4 (ex 678) (5/29); back to mainland on No. W14 (ex W4) in 1936; cut up in 1963 on No. 32635.

No. 1008 (Brighton No. 986) – new on No. 655 (10/12); to IoW on No. W9 (ex B650) (5/30); back to mainland on No. W9 in 1936; now preserved on No. 54 *Waddon*.

No. 1128 – new on No. 650 (5/20); to IoW as spare and fitted to No. W13 (ex W3) 5/32; back to mainland on No. W13 in 1949; now preserved on No. 2678.

No. 1226 – to IoW new, and first fitted to No. W8 (ex W2); to No. W11 (6/39); back to mainland on No. W11 in 1947; cut up in 1963 on No. DS681.

There are now two 'A1X' boilers on the Isle of Wight:

No. W8 has boiler No. 1012;
New on *Fenchurch* (4/13), to No. 32646 (2/58).

No. 11 has boiler No. 967:
New on No. 653 (5/12), to No. 2678 (7/37), to No. 32661 (2/54), to No. 32640 (11/58).

The sequences of boilers carried by each of the Island Terriers, while running as an 'A1X', are given below:

(Brighton boiler numbers are given, with Eastleigh numbers in brackets afterwards, where applicable).

| Loco | Boilers |
|---|---|
| W8 | boiler 1226 (4/32), 1014 (12/37), 1170 (12/51), 1012 (2/58) |
| W9 | boiler 1128 (5/20), 986 (1008) (5/30), 1014 (2/52), 964 (2/57), 935 (553) (3/63) |
| W10 | boiler 1094 (4/30) |
| W11 | boiler 1111 (7/18), 1014 (12/27), 934 (186) (7/33), 1226 (6/39), 1237 (2/56), 967 (11/58) |
| W12 | boiler 1094 (7/16), 1111 (12/29) |
| W13 | boiler 934 (186) (11/11), 1128 (5/32), 935 (553) (9/52), 1014 (8/57) |
| W14 | boiler 935 (553) (11/11), 951 (965) (5/29), 967 (7/37), 1032 (7/53), 1128 (9/59) |